Welcoming Practices

Welcoming Practices

*Creating Schools that Support
Students and Families in Transition*

Ron Avi Astor
Linda Jacobson
Stephani L. Wrabel
Rami Benbenishty

AND

Diana Pineda

OXFORD
UNIVERSITY PRESS

OXFORD
UNIVERSITY PRESS

Oxford University Press is a department of the University of Oxford. It furthers the University's objective of excellence in research, scholarship, and education by publishing worldwide. Oxford is a registered trade mark of Oxford University Press in the UK and certain other countries.

Published in the United States of America by Oxford University Press
198 Madison Avenue, New York, NY 10016, United States of America.

CIP data is on file at the Library of Congress
ISBN 978–0–19–084551–3

9 8 7 6 5 4 3 2

Printed by Sheridan Books, Inc., United States of America

This publication was developed by the USC *Welcoming Practices* team in conjunction with the *Welcoming Practices* consortium of school districts, in part, with grant funds from the U.S. Department of Defense Educational Activity (DoDEA) under award # HE125420130260248. The views expressed do not necessarily reflect the positions or policies of the DoDEA, and no official endorsement by DoDEA is intended or should be inferred.

A portion of royalties will be donated by each of the authors to educational causes related to the topics covered in the book.

Contents

Foreword

Russell J. Skiba

Students in transition are at risk for a variety of negative experiences in our schools, and their behavioral and academic outcomes are highly dependent upon the climate their school provides. The ways in which schools create a climate conducive to learning has been increasingly a topic for public debate. The 1980s and 1990s saw the rise of the philosophy and practice of zero tolerance, a policy that removed the context from disciplinary decisions. Based on broken windows theory, zero tolerance enacted a "one-size fits all" approach to discipline, applying strict penalties—primarily suspension and expulsion—for both major and minor offenses in an attempt to deter future misbehavior.

Unfortunately, the outcomes of zero tolerance were not the hoped-for increase in school safety and student discipline. Rather, research showed that schools with higher rates of exclusionary and punitive responses have less satisfactory governance, a climate that is rated more poorly by students and teachers, and decreased achievement outcomes. Moreover, those outcomes fall disproportionately upon certain students by race, gender, and sexual orientation, and those disparate rates are not due simply to socioeconomic status or higher rates of misbehavior.

In the face of these data, public policy has seen a significant shift away from zero tolerance and toward positive and preventive methods for achieving productive and healthy school climates. The federal government has issued guidance designed to shift practice away from exclusionary approaches to school discipline. At least 17 states have passed legislation reducing the use of zero tolerance–type approaches to school discipline or supporting positive alternatives. Finally, emerging research of the type highlighted by this book has begun to explore and demonstrate cost-effective, efficacious, and equitable alternatives that can help schools meet the needs of their students, especially those who are highly mobile. Among the most effective strategies for successfully shifting school climate is providing a welcoming climate at the district, school, and classroom levels.

In that context, this volume provides an invaluable resource for students and families who face increased risk due to a high rate of transition. The volume begins by defining student mobility and clarifying the risks of that mobility for students. It provides a thorough description, both through data and through the voices of students and parents, of what mobility looks like. Most importantly, it provides thorough descriptions of promising and innovative programs for providing a welcoming environment for those students and families who are in transition. It is one thing to state that schools need to be welcoming and caring for high-mobility students and families, quite another to provide a practical and evidence-based guide for implementing programs that create a climate that is supportive for students in transition.

We have learned that we cannot solve the problems that face us in schools through harsh and punitive approaches. What families and students need are effective alternatives that seek to welcome and integrate students into the school community, not push them away or push them aside. In defining the need for welcoming schools and outlining strategies for achieving that aim, the information in these pages provides a timely and much-needed addition to our knowledge base on building effective, hospitable, and safe school climates for students and families in transition.

—Professor Russell J. Skiba, Ph.D.,
Indiana University

Acknowledgments

This guide reflects many years of working with educators around the world to help create welcoming and inspiring schools.

The authors want to thank the *Building Capacity* and *Welcoming Practices* consortiums whose more than 145 schools were the source of many of the examples in this guide. The superintendents, school boards, district administrators, principals, teachers, school staff, parents, students, and hundreds of nongovernmental organizations supporting the schools were the driving forces making all this possible on the ground.

We'd like to thank our respective universities that supported this work, mainly, USC and Bar Ilan University in the most recent decade. We thank our colleagues in academia, schools, and educational organizations who have contributed to our ideas and thoughts, and the many former and current PhD students, colleagues, programmers, and undergraduates who have made this work possible. We want to thank the amazing USC and Bar Ilan Building Capacity and Welcoming Practice staff who helped compile and implement many of the ideas.

Special thanks to the numerous schools, students, educators, and families who helped us along the way and taught us so much.

We'd like to thank DoDEA's innovative partnership program for urging university-school-community partnerships to improve public schools and the lives of military children in public schools. By doing so, they have improved the lives of all students in those school districts and potentially in public schools across the United States.

Most of all, our families and friendships have propelled this work forward. We want to thank our spouses, children, grandchildren, and extended family and friends for their love and encouragement. They remind us how important this work is—creating more resources, evidence-supported interventions, ground-up participation, and strong networks of love—so that all families and schools can thrive. In the end, that is what this book is about.

May this guide be used for the betterment of the lives of students, their educators, and families by making schools supportive, caring, welcoming and lifting settings in children's lives across the world.

Introduction

There's a famous quotation that reads, "You never get a second chance to make a first impression." While the saying is usually applied to individuals, it can also be applied to how educators and staff members interact with children and families who are enrolling in their schools for the first time.

Whether students and parents feel welcomed and treated with respect can have a lasting impact on their perceptions of the school, whether they view it as a caring place, and even how students fare academically, socially, and emotionally. Teachers, administrators, and other educators in training should gain skills in how to welcome and serve children and families—not just when they walk in the door of the school or classroom, but also when they use websites and other virtual tools as well.

"I think principals and educators have to treat families like they've just checked into a 5-star hotel," writes Joe Mazza,[1] a former principal and now the leadership innovation manager at the University of Pennsylvania's Graduate School of Education. "Parents have got to feel completely comfortable and open to engaging with you, because if they come in on that first day and they don't feel that warm welcome, then the likelihood of their continuing to work with you, or digging deeper in terms of engaging with the school, goes way down" (see Figure I.1).

Transition affects all students throughout the K-12 experience—from those important first days in a kindergarten classroom to preparing for college or a career after high school. But there are many children and parents who experience school changes far more often than at those normal transition points. For those families, it is even more critical for educators to smooth their transitions into a new school, anticipate the concerns or frustrations they might have, provide academic and social-emotional support, and watch for any signs that the child is not adjusting well to the new environment.

FIGURE I.1 Yashia Vargas, a social worker in the Escondido (California) Union School District, meets with a parent in the Project SUCCESS Resource Center, which helps families in transition. Credit: Linda Jacobson.

Students who change schools often during their K-12 experience—regardless of the reasons why they transfer—don't enter new schools as a blank slate. They carry with them the impressions that have been made by previous schools, both positive and negative. As a result, teachers, administrators, and staff members might have the challenge of helping a student overcome past disappointments that took place in school. Or they might face the different challenge of living up to the expectations set by a school that a student loved and didn't want to leave.

Even if the child doesn't seem overly concerned about making new friends or understanding what is being taught in the new classroom, the child's parent might have his or her own regrets about the move or concerns about fitting into the new school community. That's why it's important for schools to consider the first impressions they're making on both students and parents.

This book reviews what researchers and educators have learned about students who transition between schools. It also provides a variety of examples of what schools are doing to support students and families going through these changes. Because many of these practices and programs have developed locally—and were created in response to specific needs—most have not been evaluated from a research perspective. It's important, however, for educators and policymakers to learn about these grass-roots efforts and for researchers to continuously examine the outcomes of promising practices and interventions.

The focus on welcoming—and on what schools do when they first meet new students and families—is in line with several other major efforts to create caring schools. These efforts include the work of the National School Climate Center,[2] the Collaborative for Academic, Social and Emotional Learning,[3] The Aspen Institute National Commission on Social, Emotional, and Academic Development,[4] and the bullying prevention work of Dr. Dorothy Espelage[5] of the University of Florida. Resiliency and transition researchers, such as Ann Masten, also influence this work.[6] This book focuses on the detailed ways that schools and other community partners can foster positive development and resiliency in the midst of a school transition. Creating "trauma-informed" or "trauma-sensitive" schools is another movement that has been active in recent years. This guide is about creating "transition-sensitive" schools and recognizing that, for some students, entering a new school and leaving behind a familiar environment can feel traumatic.

The goal is for university training programs to increase awareness of the needs of transitioning students and families among future teachers and education leaders and to highlight programs and practices that can stand as examples to other schools. This work is supported by a grant from the Department of Defense Education Activity to a Consortium of five military-connected school districts in southern California, called Welcoming Practices that Address Transition Needs of Military Students in Public Schools (*Welcoming Practices*).

Children growing up in military families certainly experience transition more than most other students and sometimes attend as many as nine schools during their K-12 years. But many other students experience transitions, and some groups of students, such as special needs students, foster care students, and homeless youth experience more school changes than others. This guide is intended to be a resource for all educators, whether or not they serve military children. The chapters highlight efforts to support transitioning students' academic as well as social-emotional needs and feature large, well-organized programs that reach many schools as well as local efforts developed by parents and teachers.

Schools handle students in transition in multiple ways—from simply assigning them to a classroom and sending them on their way to having well-established, peer support programs that help students become connected within their new school. This lack of consistency is part of the problem—and of the solution. Each school has its own unique personality, and the practices that schools use to welcome and support new students through transition will vary from school to school. There is no one *right* way to do this. But as Jane Stavem notes in her book *Student Mobility: Creating an Environment for Social and Academic Success*,[7] it's most important that schools *have a plan* in place for supporting students in transition.

There have been some efforts made to minimize school mobility among certain populations, such as homeless students and children in foster care, and to allow students to remain in their school regardless of whether they live outside of the school district's boundaries. The McKinney-Vento Homeless Education Assistance Act,[8] for example, provides funds for transportation to allow students to remain in their schools. Similarly, some states passed legislation to help avoid school transfers of foster care youth as much as possible.

But families are still going to move—sometimes for positive reasons such as better jobs and neighborhoods and sometimes due to far less pleasant circumstances, such as a divorce or an eviction. When a student changes schools, he or she is often troubled by other situations at home. "No kid moves because they wanted to," says Greg Morris, a counselor at Falcon High School, near Colorado Springs, Colorado, and the advisor for a successful student-to-student program highlighted later in this book.[9]

Schools, however, can help to ease some of the stress associated with changing schools, and more opportunities are needed to share knowledge among education professionals on how to create schools that are more welcoming and supportive of transitioning students.

Education leaders can also look outside of the K-12 system for inspiration to create practices and procedures that make newcomers feel welcome. This book draws examples from independent schools as well as from the business community to show that sometimes simple gestures can make a memorable and positive impact on new students and families.

Why Welcome?

Before focusing too much on the details of student transition and different strategies for welcoming new families, it's important to address why schools should care about presenting a welcoming environment in the first place.

Some educators might view the steps taken to welcome newcomers as a means to an end. In other words, helping new students meet friends and get involved in school activities means they will be less likely to get into trouble or skip school. Or, helping new students through the transition process means they will be less likely to fall behind academically and lose credits for graduation.

But another philosophy is that supporting students' social and emotional health—particularly during stressful events such as changing schools—is part of a school's mission, just as it is giving students a solid academic foundation.

Shana Peeples, the 2015 National Teacher of the Year, described this kind of mindset toward her profession in a Q&A when she received the honor.[10] "I represent the people who love what they do. Who are willing to do whatever it takes to help kids. Who stay after school for hours. Who steal time from their own families to help our kids. Who may be the only person that shows up at games for a kid, or at plays, at concerts," she says. "For many kids, teachers are the only person for them."

Peeples also works with a lot of students who have lived through traumatic experiences—those who are not only new to the Amarillo, Texas, school where she teaches, but have arrived there as refugees from countries in turmoil.

"The first thing to remember in working with anyone—big or small—traumatized or not, is that kindness is the first and best lesson, in my experience," she says. "It's hard to learn from someone when you're scared, so smiling is something that not only translates into any language, but also instantly sets people at ease. It begins to build trust. Once you build trust, you can begin the work of helping that child build his or her understanding and competence."

Many teachers who are recognized as outstanding—for helping students find success and reach their goals—share similar views. Rarely is high student performance the only reason that a teacher is considered excellent.

Supportive relationships between teachers and students are built into the instructional model used at Social Justice Humanitas Academy (SJHA)[11] in San Fernando, California, for example—a school that attends to students' social-emotional well-being as well as to their academic growth.

Teachers at the school "adopt" students who they think could use some extra encouragement and support, meaning that they check in with them regularly and discuss what types of resources or services students might need to be successful.

"In my role dealing with student discipline I have 'adopted' many students. I know it works," says Jeff Austin, who teaches Advanced Placement macroeconomics and American government at SJHA.[12] He's also the coordinator of testing and student discipline. "We often say that we are not teaching subjects like history, math, and English at SJHA, but that we are teaching students. I believe this and feel that it is part of my moral imperative to support my students as people first so that they can become a better student."

The strategies and ideas described throughout this book are likely to be more successful at schools where leaders and staff have a similar philosophy toward education.

Welcoming Practices

What Do We Know About Student Transition?

Understanding how changing schools affects children can help educators in their efforts to create welcoming and supportive school environments. It is also important to be aware of the different types of transitions a student may experience between prekindergarten and high school. While the purpose of this book is to highlight the different ways educators can support children and families changing schools, it's still important to look at the many reasons why they are changing.

School moves are commonly classified as one of two types: structural or nonstructural. *Structural changes* occur when students are required to switch schools because of the distinct features of or changes within the education system. The most common example of a structural change is promotional, such as when a child finishes 5th grade and goes to a new school for 6th grade. These promotional moves are typically viewed as transitions rather than school moves.

The development of new schools to address overcrowding, the rezoning of school boundaries, or the closing of low-performing schools are other examples of structural changes. While students and parents might not always feel positive about a structural move, a student tends to move with peers when these changes happen and thus is not considered a "new student."

Nonstructural mobility, on the other hand, is any school change that is not created by the features of the school system and can be the result of a multitude of life circumstances. These can include a parent's new job, a divorce, a change in custody or foster family for a child, the result of a disciplinary action at a school, or a conflict with a teacher or another student.

Students may also switch schools because they—or their parents—are seeking a specific type of academic program, such as a magnet program or a charter school. According to Dr. Russell Rumberger[1] at the University of California Santa Barbara, 60%

of students nationally make unscheduled school changes at some point between kindergarten and 12th grade. A smaller proportion of students experience many more of these changes.

The scientific literature shows that both promotional and nonpromotional changes may create challenges. Moves from prekindergarten to kindergarten and then to 1st grade, then the move to middle school, and from middle school to high school are all accompanied by changes in relationships with teachers and peers and in academic expectations.

Whether a student changes schools once or several times during his or her K-12 education, support from adults and other students may be needed for the student to integrate into the new community and excel academically, socially, and behaviorally. If a student is trying to start over in a new school after experiencing bullying in a previous site, for example, that student might have a greater need for programs that can help him or her form new friendships and get involved in school activities. The remainder of this chapter looks at what researchers have discovered about who is moving, where they move, and what these moves mean for the students making the changes.

Trends in Transition

There are some demographic trends in which students are making unscheduled school moves during the academic year or in multiple academic years. For example, studies have found that students in the elementary grades switch more often than students enrolled in middle or high schools.[2]

An overwhelming body of research also documents that school changes occur more often among certain demographic groups.[3] These are:

- students from low-income families
- students receiving special education services
- students with disabilities
- Latino students
- African-American students
- English-language learners

Students from low-income families and students from historically underserved racial or ethnic groups, such as Latino and African-American students, are also more likely to make multiple moves in a year or in consecutive years. Students located in urban areas make more school changes than those in suburban and rural communities. Finally, low-performing students also typically make unscheduled school changes more often than those who are doing well academically.

There are also specific communities of students who are more mobile than others. These include individuals experiencing homelessness, children of military-connected families, students living in foster care, and students from migrant families.[4] For example, military-connected students change schools, on average, six to nine times between kindergarten and high school graduation, and students in the New York City foster care system report moving more than twice as often once in the system than they did in the year prior to placement in foster care.[5] Like their nonmobile peers, highly mobile students all have diverse needs, abilities, and prior experiences. Recognizing these unique characteristics is all part of supporting students and their families in the transition to a new school community.

Understanding Student Mobility

School mobility refers to the proportion of a school's enrollment that changes during the school year. On average, urban schools have the highest rates of turnover—33%.[6] In suburban areas, mobility rates are at 22% and in rural communities at 16%. These changes include students who leave the school mid-year as well as new students arriving after the year begins. In Massachusetts, for example, the average enrollment turnover in the state was 10.3% in 2009, but some schools reported a more than 60% enrollment change in the same year.[7]

Researchers find that the majority of students who move make school transfers within the same district, even when the moves are nonstructural.[8] When a student remains within the same district, there may be less adjustment to school rules and regulations; increased continuity with textbooks, curriculums, and courses; and added comfort with the community surrounding the school.

In other words, a child who makes a local transition may experience less disruption and anxiety than one who moves to a school in another district, region, state, or country. Students who come from low-income families as well as African-American and Latino students tend to move within their district more than do other groups. By contrast, white students and those from more economically advantaged families are more likely to move to a school in a different district, researchers have found.[9]

The Changing Conversation About Mobility

Early discussions about student mobility—before 1980—characterized the changing of homes and schools as positive events. The assumption was that families were seeking better economic and educational opportunities that could benefit the school-aged children in the family. But, more recently, with the advent of more rigorous ways to study mobility—and improvements in how districts handle student records—this perspective has shifted.

Now, school changes that occur within a district are more often viewed as disruptive to a student's academic life. Transitions to schools in different districts are now the moves that are classified as more advantageous and assumed to be for the purposes of securing a higher quality or better-fitting school for a student.[10] More research in this area is needed, but it's still worth noting that just because a child moves into a new school in a nice neighborhood doesn't mean he or she won't need some support during the process.

Proactive Versus Reactive

In recent years, trends in student mobility have been influenced by the growth of charter schools, magnet programs, and the push for universal prekindergarten. Students moving to a charter or magnet school within their own district are often seeking a specific type of learning or educational experience. These are considered "proactive" moves and may relate to academic outcomes in ways that differ from traditional within-district moves that are viewed as "reactive."

The push to increase young children's access to early-learning programs is largely viewed as a positive development in the United States, allowing children to develop the preacademic and social-emotional skills they will need for today's more rigorous kindergarten classrooms. Roughly 70% of four-year-olds in the United States now attend some type of preschool program—either public or private—according to the National Center for Education Statistics.[11]

But attending prekindergarten can also add one more transition in the life of a young child. For example, if a student gets a spot in a public prekindergarten program, his or her class might not be in the same school that the child will attend for kindergarten, based on school attendance boundaries. In addition, since many prekindergarten programs are only half-day, children often are attending more than one center- or home-based program before kindergarten. This means the child is leaving behind two familiar settings when he or she starts kindergarten. Chapter 6 will take a closer look at practices that help young children adjust to a new school.

The Effects of Transition on Students

Researchers have examined several aspects of a student's educational experience following a move. Mobility is a difficult topic to study, in part because highly mobile students are more likely to have incomplete academic records. More information on the role of state data systems is available in Chapter 2. Below are some overall findings regarding how students are affected by changing schools.

Academic

Research on student mobility suggests that school changes are harmful to a student's academic progress.[12] The first reason is simply because, in the process of moving during the school year, a child might miss some days of school. There are also numerous anecdotal stories from school officials who have talked about families not showing up to register for school until after Labor Day, even if school started in August.

When academic records do not arrive in a timely fashion or are incomplete, schools struggle to identify appropriate class placements, determine credit transfers, and provide necessary or required support services for the new student, according to a 2010 report from the US Government Accountability Office. On average, research[13] suggests a single school move costs a student 10 days of instruction, with each move increasing these gaps in a student's learning. Some researchers[14] suggest that mobility helps explain, in part, the achievement gaps many current education policies are aiming to reduce.

Research shows that, compared to students who don't change schools often, mobile students show lower academic achievement in both math and reading following a school transition.[15] Research consistently suggests that the more frequently a student moves or the more a student moves over a number of years, the lower the student's academic performance in math and reading.

Some researchers say that a one-time unscheduled school move does not have a negative impact on a child's school performance, but it's clear that numerous transitions in a short period of time are related to lower achievement.

The educational disruption associated with mobility not only affects children who are changing schools, but also impacts their stable classmates. A 2011 study led by Stephen Raudenbush[16] at the University of Chicago showed that stable students enrolled in a highly mobile school are predicted to be one month behind in academic content coverage for each year enrolled in that school.

Integrating new students into a classroom may interrupt the instruction received by all students since a teacher might repeat a lesson or topic area. Strict pacing guides tend to limit the flexibility a teacher has to cover material more than once, but he or she might still ask a student in the class to spend some time helping the new student catch up. Having a plan for attending to the challenges and disruptions associated with mobility—as Stavem[17] suggests—can benefit all students in a school, not just those who are new.

Some research finds that highly mobile students are at a higher risk of repeating a grade compared to those who have not changed schools.[18] And a 2004 study led by Diana Gruman[19] at Western Washington University showed that mobile students showed declines in classroom participation, which includes actions such as listening while others speak and cooperating with other students during group activities.

Attendance

Consistent attendance leads to positive academic outcomes for students, both in terms of grade point average and standardized test scores, research shows.[20] Researchers have found connections between unscheduled school changes and lower attendance rates.[21] These school absences are above and beyond the learning time a student misses while transitioning from one school to another. Absenteeism rates among mobile students are higher at the high school level than in the elementary grades. And research has shown that a high rate of absenteeism is considered a risk factor for a student dropping out of high school.[22]

Social

Not surprisingly, students who make mid-year school transitions tend to be less engaged in extracurricular activities at their new school, research shows.[23] Transitioning to a new school means more than just changes in the learning environment. A student's social and peer group is also affected. A student who was involved in after-school programs, sports, or clubs at his or her prior school might not have an opportunity to get involved in similar activities at the new school because of organizational rules or deadlines.

Research[24] from the early 1990s suggested that mobile students may have fewer contacts with friends and fewer close relationships than their stable counterparts. However, the increased use of social media and technology in the past two decades has likely had a profound effect on mobile students' capacity to maintain relationships with friends from previous schools and communities. Recent studies on school transitions have not looked at the social networks of mobile students.

But even if mobile students are now able to maintain relationships with friends from prior schools, there is some evidence to suggest that they may still have smaller social circles in the new school. Mobile students have reported struggling to make friends even after nine months following a school move. This suggests that it's important for educators to follow-up with new students in a school—not just after a few weeks, but also throughout the school year. Strategies for monitoring how a student is adjusting are covered in Chapter 10.

Research[25] on middle and high school students suggests that those who make a residential move are more likely to associate with peers who skip school, are less engaged in school, get lower grades, and experiment with smoking and drinking alcohol. While only one-third of school changes are associated with changes to a student's home address, this research provides potential insight into the peer networks of students following a school change and reinforces the need for educators to pay attention to the friendships students are forming in their new school.

Behavioral

The bulk of research on student mobility focuses on academic outcomes. Less is known about the behavioral dimensions of a student's experience. The studies that have looked at the relationship between mobility and behavior, however, show consistent trends. Mobile students are more likely than stable students to receive at least one suspension (in- or out-of-school). Suspension rates are particularly high for students who enroll in several different schools within one year.[26] One study[27] showed that highly mobile students—those who make three or more school changes—are at an elevated risk for emotional or behavioral problems and are more likely to receive psychological support services than are stable students. Research[28] also finds that a student who changes schools following an expulsion is at the highest risk for poor academic outcomes.

Promotional Transition

While most research on student mobility focuses on those students making nonstructural changes, some studies also focus on how students fare after a structural transition, such as from elementary to middle school or middle to high school. Promotional changes, like nonpromotional school changes, can have implications for students' academic performance in the year of the transition as well as in the years following the school change.

Scheduled transitions, such as the one between elementary and middle school, can be difficult. Students experience change not only in how the school operates, but also in social roles. Middle schools are often larger, more impersonal, and more academically challenging than elementary schools. A student, for example, might see a big jump in the amount of homework assigned each night. Relationships with teachers and peers can undergo many stressful changes, and students worry more about whether they are accepted or rejected by their peers. Researchers say that this transition has been associated with psychological distress, lower self-esteem, adjustment problems, declines in academic motivation and achievement, and increases in discipline problems.[29]

A study[30] focusing on a small number of districts found that when students had to make a school change between 5th and 6th grades, those students demonstrated lower achievement in 6th grade than students who were in schools with a K-8 configuration. The same study suggests that students also demonstrate lower achievement following a promotional transition to high school. Achievement in 9th grade was lower for students who made a 6th-grade promotional change than for the students who attended K-8 schools. More recent research[31] confirms that making a promotional school change after the elementary grades—in either the 6th or 7th grade—is associated with lower achievement following the transition, especially for students who demonstrated lower achievement prior to the school change.

Conclusion

While there is still much to learn about student mobility, it's clear that school changes have real consequences for students in both the short- and long-term. An awareness of these trends—and the multiple ways that mobility can affect students—can help educators and others who work with schools develop strategies to support students making a transition and hopefully prevent a student from feeling isolated or making poor choices.

The following chapters look at the importance of student data systems and share the voices of parents and students about their experiences in new schools. The remainder of the book examines the variety of innovative programs, services, and strategies that can help create schools that are more welcoming and sensitive to the needs of mobile students.

Mobility in Student Data Systems

For schools to be more proactive about addressing the needs of transitioning students and families, it's important that district officials have a good sense of how often students are changing schools, who these students are, where they're coming from, and where they're going.

Currently, there is wide variation in how states handle mobility in their student data systems.[1] While some states have a specific definition of mobility, there are also differences in those definitions. By law, states track migrant and homeless students, but not all flag other groups of students that are likely to be mobile, such as military-connected students or those in foster care.

Another complication is that when students move, schools do not mark the reason for the transition. Without knowing the reason for the change, all mobile students are lumped into one category—movers. But, as the previous chapter showed, the circumstances surrounding a move can affect students in different ways and have implications for how schools respond.

If a move is proactive, for example, the family and the child may feel less stress and the student might feel more positive about the experience. If the change into a new school is reactive—caused perhaps by a difficult financial situation or leaving a negative situation at another school—the student and parents might feel more anxiety about the new school and need additional support and friendship during that time.

Current data systems and the information they provide make it very difficult for researchers to separate the effect of the school move from the effect of the circumstances surrounding the move. These are important distinctions for educators to consider.

Data systems do allow for researchers and practitioners to understand if a student moved during the summer or during the academic year. The timing of moves may be suggestive of the type of move a student is making; proactive moves may be more likely to occur in the summer months when learning will not be disrupted. Mid-year moves may have a proactive element, such as families moving for a better job, but they may also be reactive in nature, such as a loss of housing.

So while the timing of a school change may provide some context, timing does not provide the whole picture of what a mobile student is experiencing. The research on mobility has largely looked at the relationships between mobility and the academic, social, and behavioral aspects of schooling rather than establishing the effect of mobility on these outcomes.

In some states, mobility is considered an issue that deserves more attention in student data systems. Colorado, for example, provides detailed mobility and stability rates. The District of Columbia public schools include "student movement" as part of student equity reports. And some states, such as Illinois, also require mobility rates to be included on school report cards.

As student data systems become increasingly sophisticated, states and districts will be able to ask better questions about patterns of movement among students, says Elizabeth Dabney, the associate director for research and policy analysis at the Data Quality Campaign.

The "mindset" of education leaders also makes a difference in whether mobility is considered an issue that could be affecting student outcomes, Dabney adds. "It's whether they view data as being in service of students and families or if they're more in compliance mode," she says.

Asking better questions about mobile students and the ways in which mobility affects important outcomes like achievement and the persistence to college and careers is not enough. States must be intentional about the type of information and the quality of data collected so that these important questions can be answered. Otherwise, a state's or school's capacity to do something meaningful to address the challenges associated with mobility will continue to be limited.

In recent years, advocacy organizations and researchers have used data to raise awareness about student mobility in particular geographic areas and the impact it has on students' success in school. These are examples of how quality data can provide educators and families with a better understanding of what mobility means for a student.

Ohio

In 2012, the Thomas B. Fordham Institute worked with Community Research Partners, based in Columbus, Ohio,[2] to better understand the extent of student mobility throughout that state. The report was one attempt to address what the authors called a "cavernous void in school mobility research." Data were analyzed from all 609 of the state's school districts, and additional profiles were completed on large urban areas in the state. In Cincinnati, for example, the researchers found that in those districts with the highest mobility, one of every three students in a school at the start of the school year is not in the same school at the end of the year.

As other studies have, the Ohio report also found a link between high mobility and low student performance. In the Cincinnati public schools, for example, students who moved (during the year or over the summer, once, twice, and three or more times) performed significantly lower on 3rd- and 8th-grade state tests in both math and reading than students who had never moved.

Massachusetts

In Massachusetts,[3] the Rennie Center for Education Research and Policy issued a 2011 report focusing on student mobility in that state, with a particular focus on rates in what are considered the state's "gateway cities." In some of the districts in those cities, nearly one-third of students change schools during the course of the school year.

Faculty and staff members interviewed as part of the study said that addressing the problems associated with mobility are a high priority but that the challenges are very difficult to overcome and schools and districts don't usually have the capacity to address those challenges. Classroom teachers are often not equipped to respond to the "diverse and complex needs that mobile students present," the report says. Schools may not have specialists who can provide individual academic support to students who are grade levels behind, and many don't have social workers who can link families to other services in the community.

The report also notes that funding for schools for the following year is typically determined by an attendance count in the fall and doesn't adjust for students who might come into the school after that date and have different educational needs, such as special education students or English-language learners. "When students join after the school year has already begun, the staffing allocation doesn't change," said one principal quoted in the report. "Often times we get students who require SPED or ELL services, but there's no increase in staffing for them."

Tennessee

Finally, the Tennessee Consortium on Research, Evaluation, and Development[4] recently released a study on mobility in the state's Achievement School District (ASD), which is charged with improving student outcomes in the lowest performing 5% of schools in the state. In the 2013–14 school year, there were 17 schools in the ASD—most of them in Memphis. The researchers wanted to gain a better understanding of student mobility and the patterns of movement in and out of these schools since they were no longer being managed by a local district.

Initially, student mobility rates in the ASD schools were similar to or slightly higher than those of other low-performing schools. But once the schools became part of the ASD, mobility rates dropped in some schools. For the first cohort of six schools in the ASD, the rate dropped from 46% in the 2011–12 school year to 37% in 2013–14. In future years, the researchers will look more closely at the performance of the ASD schools and how it is affected by students moving in and out of these schools.

Accountability and Teacher Effectiveness Systems

The authors of the Massachusetts report discuss another challenge related to mobility—the inability of education accountability systems, whether at the state level or as part of federal legislation, to consider that many schools are serving a student body that is constantly changing. Superintendents interviewed for the report said they don't think high mobility should be used as an excuse, but they did think the performance of mobile and non-mobile students should be examined separately.

With more states now tying teacher evaluation in part to academic performance, student mobility also plays a role in whether teachers are considered "effective" under some states' value-added rating systems. This work is still in its early stages, and many states are still creating rules for establishing a student's "teacher of record" for evaluation purposes. A document from the U.S. Department of Education's Reform Support Network[5] reviewed how some winners of Race to the Top grants were approaching the issue. The District of Columbia public schools, for example "weights value-added analysis by the fraction of the year a student spends with a particular teacher," the document says. The Illinois State Board of Education encourages school districts to include as many students as possible, and, in Colorado's system, student mobility is considered when examining how much growth a teacher's students have made. Some states reviewed, however, still don't have any rules regarding mobility.

Whether it's fair to hold schools and teachers responsible for students who were in their classrooms for only part of the year—especially students who arrived during the year—is a topic of considerable debate. But it does give schools and teachers an additional reason to create welcoming environments and provide the support students need in order to do well after changing schools.

Understanding Root Causes

When schools experience high mobility, it's also important to examine the issue in the larger context of what is happening in the community as a whole. In other words, what is the reason that a student has to move?

For example, in Baltimore's Brooklyn and Curtis Bay neighborhoods, many families were at risk of becoming homeless—a situation that likely would have resulted in the children having to change schools. So the schools in those areas worked with the United Way of Central Maryland's Family Stability Initiative to keep some families in their homes or find other housing that would keep them from being placed in a shelter.[6]

In California, many schools serve children from migrant families. Two organizations—the Center for Farmworker Families and Human Agenda—want to change a law that allows migrant farmworkers to live in a migrant camp only between May and November.[7] Currently, in order to return to the camp the following year, the workers and their families must move at least 50 miles away. This means that children are leaving school before the end of the academic year and returning to that school well after the new school year has started. The organizations are lobbying for a change that would allow families to find housing outside of the camp and keep their children in the same schools all year.

As Dabney says, data systems will increasingly be able to help educators answer questions about when and why students are moving so that schools can create routines for assisting families through transition periods. Raising awareness of how changing schools impacts a child's education can also lead to creative solutions for smoothing those transitions or limiting them as much as possible.

The Voices of Students and Parents

In addition to analyzing data on which students are moving and how often, educators can learn about the circumstances, needs, and experiences of new families and students by asking them directly.

Online customer satisfaction surveys are becoming more common in school districts. District and school leaders are asking parents and students to rate their performance in a variety of areas, from their communication practices to the classroom environment.

A 2013 report from Hanover Research[1] suggests that these surveys coincide with the increasing level of competition in education spurred by the growing number of charter school options, magnet schools, and open enrollment policies in many districts.

"As school attendance in charter and magnet settings is not determined by geographic boundaries, such schools must make efforts to satisfy parent and student 'customers' to ensure robust enrollments," the report says.

These surveys also show evidence of the influence that the business world has had on the education field. Business practices that can help schools improve the way they welcome new families will be discussed in Chapter 8, but it's clear that schools are thinking more about how they serve students and their parents.

While the use of surveys is growing, it's far less common for districts to ask for feedback specifically about their enrollment procedures or how the schools handle the issue of transition in general.

Survey Says . . .

As part of the *Welcoming Practices* initiative, the Consortium districts surveyed parents to gather input on topics such as the registration process, the responsiveness of the staff, and the interest shown in meeting students' individual needs.[2] More than 1,400 parent responses were received, representing 2,300 children. On a 5-point scale, the parents indicated their level of agreement with statements such as:

- The school made my child feel like he/she was part of the school community.
- The school helped my child connect with other students.
- The school helped me connect to other families.
- The school helped connect me to services and resources in the community.

The parents responded that, overall, they and their children felt welcomed by the school, giving ratings above a 4. But the ratings were lower—closer to a 3—on whether the school attempted to connect them with other families or refer them to any specific programs or activities their child might need or want.

Because the survey was conducted in districts serving a large population of military children and families, parents with a military connection were asked to provide comments on their perceptions of how welcoming the school staff members were toward them and their children. Their views obviously reflect their military experiences, which include the added stress caused by having a parent deployed during wartime. But it's easy to see how some of the statements could come from any parent whose child has attended a lot of schools.

"The teacher nor the principal took any consideration that my son was bounced around from school to school since kindergarten," one parent wrote. Another said, "There is a lack of support, understanding, or compassion for children who move a lot due to life in the military."

Others, however, reported being treated with respect and kindness. One parent described an experience that seems out of the ordinary: "The principal met with me personally, and allowed me to share my child's background and strengths with him. This direct interaction enabled him to suggest the most optimal placement for my child, and gave me a sense of assurance that our principal *cared* for the specific needs of my child," the parent wrote. "He gave us a guided tour of the facility, and shared with us exciting opportunities available during the school year . . . this gave my child something to look forward to while she anticipated the start of the school year, and a sense of satisfaction in 'finding her place' amidst the student population at school."

The School Office: Making or Breaking a New Family's Experience

Several respondents in the *Welcoming Practices* survey shared comments focusing on their interactions with school office staff members. The comments indicate that a lot is riding on those initial experiences in the school office and that parents' and students' judgments of the school they are entering are heavily influenced by those initial meetings or requests for information. See Figure 3.1. As one parent said, "A receptionist is

FIGURE 3.1 A school office. Credit: Natex Architects.

the first person you meet when you walk through the doors of the school and can set a positive tone for the school if she has good manners.".

Here are some examples of comments from parents who reported unpleasant experiences in the school office:

- "When my daughter, her father, and I first visited the school in order to enroll her, the receptionist wasn't friendly and portrayed an arrogant attitude."
- "It is unfortunate that their secretaries are so rude and are the first encounter with parents registering their students at the school."
- "We appreciate almost all of the teachers that we have had . . . , however, the front office staff is very rude and not helpful. They are too busy doing other parts of their jobs that they do not acknowledge parents and they act as if you are 'putting them out' when you ask for something."
- "I felt they were rude, ignored us, and didn't want to deal with us merely because we had yet to receive our first gas bill." (A gas or other utility bill is often required to establish residency within a district.)
- "When they do finally ask what you need, they are generally rude and unpleasant. I dread going to the office for anything, and my kids are afraid of the staff, so I usually have to do all interactions."

As mentioned in the introduction, a parent's view of how he or she is being received and treated in a school office is often colored by his or her experiences in a past school. And it may be that someone is perceived as "rude" because he or she wouldn't make an exception to district policies regarding enrollment procedures or required documents.

But schools that want to create a welcoming environment recognize the stress that parents are experiencing when they move. They hire staff members who are customer service–oriented or provide training to improve the office atmosphere.

In several additional comments, other parents conveyed that being warmly welcomed by office staff members contributed to a positive transition into the school:

- "When selecting an elementary school for my children, I visited a few and one stood out above and beyond the others. From the moment you walk into the doors . . . you feel welcome. The front office staff was friendly, outgoing, and warm."
- "We were in the process of moving from Hawaii to California, and the receptionist was fantastic in answering all our questions. She was friendly and very helpful. When we arrived in California and went to the school to turn in paperwork, she made us feel like we were friends. Great Job!! Thank you."
- "Very welcoming front office, always friendly. Everyone you asked was very helpful and willing to help. At times you did not have to ask; people would see you and ask if you needed help."

Other parents commented on how the principal can add to or take away from creating a welcoming environment:

- "We love the visibility of the principal in the mornings and afternoons. She always has a warm smile on her face even when faced with a complaint."
- "He hides away in his office the moment parents walk through the door; he makes no effort to be friendly and get to know the children at the school."

Comments from parents also show that being friendly is not enough. They want school staff members to provide information or at least point them in the right direction:

- "They were friendly, but no one asked if I had any questions."
- "People were generally friendly. However, there was no information given to either of us about school programs, district policies, or community involvement. We were basically told that they didn't have a program for her academic needs and just given an enrollment packet."

Students' Views

Parents' experiences with registering for school are an important part of the transition process for a family. But, for this guidebook, input from students who have changed schools was also gathered to find out what they liked and didn't like about how the schools handled the experience.

Even if parents take steps to tour the new school or seek out situations in which their children can meet potential classmates, students are still on their own in those first few days and weeks. Survey questions asked students what they liked and didn't like about their initial experiences in their new school and whether the school provided them with information, gave them a tour of the school, or paired them with another student during the first few days.

Conducting a survey such as this is a way for schools to monitor their efforts to be welcoming and to see whether the programs they have created are making the transition process for students easier. Appendix B provides examples of surveys that administrators can use or adapt for their own school communities.

Interviews with a few students who have experienced school changes other than just moving from elementary to middle or middle to high school also provide greater detail. The students were asked what they thought schools handled well and what made them feel uncomfortable or unwelcome.

Eraina

Eraina has attended five schools—one elementary, two middle schools, and two high schools.[3] At the second middle school she attended, all of the incoming students were grouped together for initial orientation activities, separate from the students who were returning to the school.

"This was really helpful because it minimized a lot of the pressure. We were all new, we were all lost, we were all nervous, and we were all essentially friendless. It was a relief to be with people who understood what it was like to be new," Eraina says. "A lot of schools try to integrate you with the kids who have grown up in the district. In theory that seems like a good idea, but in reality it makes things uncomfortable because often times they have their own friends and aren't really concerned about the new student. This is isolating and, for me at least, makes me feel like a third wheel whenever I'm around them."

Eraina also remembers moments during which she felt completely lost in a new classroom and wishes teachers would have taken the time to explain their routine.

"Recently I had a teacher who didn't explain to me how he structured his class, and one day he said, 'Okay, time to turn in your portfolio complete with an essay plan for your test' and I was empty handed. I had no idea that he expected a portfolio, and I had no idea that there would be an essay on the test," Eraina says. "Instantly what was once an 'A' mark in that subject became a 'D' mark because I had no idea what was expected of me. The key to a smooth academic transition is communication. The teacher taking time to pull you aside, explain what's going on and what the class is learning, how the assignments work, etc., makes a class a whole lot less scary."

Paige

When Paige moved during her high school years, she found it helpful to look for an elective with a lot of participants. She chose Junior ROTC.[4] "There you have a lot of leadership and team bonding that helps force you to branch out and meet people with at least one thing in common with you."

What she didn't like was trying to navigate the time out of class on her own. "I didn't like going to the lunchroom by myself and looking for a place to sit. Everyone had their spot or group of friends, and it is very intimidating walking into a large lunchroom all by yourself," she says. "It was also difficult trying to find my class, and once that challenge was over, trying to find a seat with someone who looked 'nice' or 'accepting' was always nerve-wracking. In most public schools, kids have been friends since the 'sandbox' days. It's awkward and intimidating to go up to a bunch of girls who have 'inside jokes' that date back to years ago."

These students' comments likely reflect the types of experiences and emotions many students have when they enter new schools. Asking newcomers for their input on what works and doesn't work for them can help schools improve the way they connect with students during those first few weeks.

Every Move Is Different

Listening to parents' and students' voices shows that not everyone handles the challenges that come with transition in the same way. A child who changed schools without any problems one year might struggle if he or she has to change schools and neighborhoods again a few years later.

"You can't look at a child and say, 'You did so great two years ago. What's your problem now?'" says Sally Patterson, who conducts training workshops for the Military Child Education Coalition.[5] She adds, for example, that a student who moved willingly in the 7th grade might have a first boyfriend or girlfriend in the 10th grade and feel angry—even bitter—about having to start over in a new school. In addition, two children from the same family can handle changing schools in very different ways. One might run right out on the playground and join in whatever game is being played, while the other is sitting alone, wishing to be back at the previous school.

Children in general are viewed as resilient—able to recover from disappointments and adjust to changes in their lives. But experts say resilience isn't necessarily a natural trait; it's something that needs to be encouraged and can be built through supportive relationships and experiences that allow children to develop self-confidence and to connect with others.

According to the Center on the Developing Child at Harvard University, the "single most common factor for children who develop resilience is at least one stable and committed relationship with a supportive parent, caregiver, or other adult."[6]

Research on children in military families—who change schools more often than most students—also provides some insight that can help educators build resilience in any student who has changed schools frequently. A 2013 issue of *The Future of Children* summarized studies on the well-being of military children after a move. One study, for example, found that children who bounced back the quickest after relocating had specific characteristics including an "internal locus of control," optimism and good health, both physically and mentally.

BOX 3.1 Seven Factors That Can Help Young People Develop Resilience

Pediatrician Dr. Kenneth Ginsberg of the Children's Hospital of Philadelphia names seven factors that allow young people to be resilient when they experience difficult circumstances. This is from his website—www.fosteringresilience.com/7cs_professionals.php:

Competence: When we notice what young people are doing right and give them opportunities to develop important skills, they feel competent.

Confidence: Young people need confidence to be able to navigate the world, think outside the box, and recover from challenges.

Connection: Connections with other people, schools, and communities offer young people the security that allows them to stand on their own and develop creative solutions.

Character: Young people need a clear sense of right and wrong and a commitment to integrity.

Contribution: Young people who contribute to the well-being of others will receive gratitude rather than condemnation and learn that contributing feels good.

Coping: Young people with a variety of healthy coping strategies will be less likely to turn to dangerous quick fixes when stressed.

Control: Young people who understand privileges and respect are earned through demonstrated responsibility will learn to make wise choices and feel a sense of control.

The Center on the Developing Child's work on resilience supports the link between physical activity and resilience. "Age-appropriate, health-promoting activities can significantly improve the odds that an individual will recover from stress-inducing experiences," they write. "For example, regular physical exercise, stress-reduction practices, and programs that actively build executive function and self-regulation skills can improve the abilities of children and adults to cope with, adapt to, and even prevent adversity in their lives." See Box 3.1, which describes seven factors that can help young people develop resilience.

Studies involving military families have also shown that children have an easier time adjusting to a new home and school when mothers feel positive about the changes.[7] These findings support the concept that schools should focus their welcoming activities on both students and parents. Military children and parents in a school can also be a great resource for other families who have less experience with school transitions.

Making Virtual Connections

A student's transition into a school starts well before he or she walks through the front doors or sits down at a desk. There are multiple strategies schools can use to smooth students' transition and make families feel welcome before they arrive at the school. Since many of these strategies involve technology, they are presented in their own chapter.

The first impression many schools leave on incoming families takes place in front of a computer, tablet screen, or mobile phone—not face-to-face. When a family is moving to a new community, one of the first things many parents—and students—will do is search online for the district or school and try to gather some basic information about the enrollment process, the neighborhood, and the achievement scores.

"During my most recent move, I spent time on the school website to get a feel of how the school ran and what classes were available," says Eraina, a student featured in Chapter 3.[1] "This was helpful and made the transition not so shocking and confusing."

Parents might also search for information on courses or activities for their children and even read teacher profiles if those are available. Parents want to cushion the transition process for their children as much as possible; they want to be able to answer their children's questions about the new school.

School and district websites don't, however, always make that process simple. Sometimes registration information is not easily found on a homepage, and parents might end up on pages that say "under construction" when they try to dig for more details. Some schools and districts provide email addresses for key staff members; others don't. And, sometimes, staff members have left their position or the district, but their contact information is not updated.

School Webmasters is a Mesa, Arizona-based company that develops and administers websites for schools and districts.[2] A December 2014 blog post on the company's site entitled "Do Parents Use Your Website?" offered this advice:

In this digital age, parents looking to find a school for their child are likely to visit your website before ever visiting your campus. Does your website provide the answers they're looking for? Prospective families look for:

- information about your school's curriculum, programs, and staff;
- photos that illustrate the general climate of your campus;
- self-explanatory, printable online registration forms, and
- updated tuition/fee schedules.

These days, parents are also likely to want to enroll and pay fees online. Does your website have these functionalities? If not, it may be costing you student enrollment you didn't even know you were losing.

This chapter presents a variety of examples of how schools and districts are using technology to connect and support new families. Some of these are minor additions to existing websites, and others require more expertise in mobile communications. The important thing is to prominently and clearly display any information for incoming families on the school's or district's homepage. As immigrant populations continue to increase in the nation's school districts, it's also important to provide website information in the languages spoken in that community. Chapter 7 provides more details on ways that schools are serving families who are transitioning from other countries.

Welcoming Practices Consortium

Using technology to engage and welcome new families is a primary component of the *Welcoming Practices* grant involving the University of Southern California (USC) and five military-connected school districts in southern California. As part of the grant, the team created a mobile app—WelConnect—that links families to the district, school, community, and military resources matching their needs and interests long before they even move into the area.[3] The purpose of the app, pictured in Figure 4.1, is to help families make a smooth transition into their new schools and communities. It also gives educators and local organizations a way to let families know what services and programs are available. A school social worker, for example, can help a new family find child care in their neighborhood, an after-school program for one of their children, and tutoring support for another. A student study team can help educators look for available resources for a particular student so that referrals can be made. Having an app with links to all the available resources saves families time and helps them feel at home more quickly.

Designed for both Android and iOS devices, the app allows users to search for the local resources and programs they need near their local school, save them as favorites

FIGURE 4.1 WelConnect.

for easy reference, and find them on a map. Based on a deep understanding of students' and families' needs, the app has predefined "tags" so that searches are more efficient. The resources are organized into groups, such as tutoring, mental health programs, child care, religious and spiritual support, and many more. The parent (or educator) can choose to look for resources in the child's school, district, or even in the community, mapping the desired resources in their neighborhood.

Each resource comes with details such as contact information, a web link, and directions. Educators and service providers in the community are also able to use the app when looking for programs to help families and students. A hospital social worker who is discharging a student patient, for example, can use the app to look for follow-up resources for the child in his or her school, district, or neighborhood. This may replace hours of Internet searches and phone calls. Over time, districts will be better informed about what incoming families need and want for their children and will make sure that these resources are available and accessible to families.

WelConnect is also intended to serve as a model to other districts. While many are now creating apps, incorporating connections to community providers takes this concept to the next level.

Online Registration

Apart from *Welcoming Practices*, districts across the country are increasingly shifting much, if not all, of the registration process to the Web. In some districts, once the process is complete, the parent prints a confirmation page and the student turns it in on the first day of class. In other districts, the process can be begun online and completed in person.

What's clear, however, is that shifting to online forms should not make the process more cumbersome for families transferring into a district. In the survey responses, parents complained that sometimes districts didn't have a record of the online forms submitted or that they were still being required to complete paper versions of the same forms they completed online. Of course, glitches can be expected when any new system is being implemented, but a smooth registration process from a remote location can be the first step toward establishing a rapport with new families.

Welcoming Videos

One simple method for creating an inviting website is to develop a welcoming video that is placed on the school's homepage. This is also an excellent project for students to lead, either as part of a club activity or as an assignment that integrates technology, writing, and other academic skills. Schools could even hold a competition to choose a winning video or create a series of videos on different features of the school.

Members of a Junior Student-to-Student group at Stuart Mesa Elementary in Oceanside, California, for example, created a video that gave incoming students a glimpse into their school. (More information on Student-to-Student is provided in Chapter 5.) A video created by the Chula Vista Elementary School District,[4] for example, gives prospective families an overview of the district and some of its key initiatives for serving students and families.

Virtual Tours

School websites can also be used to give new students and families a window into your campus. Students who play an instrument, for example, would take great interest in seeing the band room in the school where they are headed. Another student might find some reassurance in seeing where he or she would stand to catch the bus to go home.

The website for the Opelika City Schools in Alabama, for example, features virtual tours of every school in the district, with some showing panoramic views of several on-campus locations, such as Opelika High School's performing arts center, football stadium, media center, cafeteria, and a chemistry class.[5] This, again, is a project that could involve students and be used to communicate their role in welcoming new students and helping them to feel a part of the school.

Frequently Asked Questions

A list of questions and answers is another simple feature that can be added to a school's or district's homepage, perhaps with a heading that reads something like: "Are you relocating to our district? Here's what you need to know."

This list could be a compilation of information that is already probably available on your site, such as important deadlines, documents required for registration, and links to after-school programs and parent organizations.

Allowing families to take care of initial registration procedures online—and anticipating the kinds of questions they will have about coming to your community—is one way to show consideration for the concerns of families that are in the midst of a transition.

Submit a Question

Another idea is to create an online form for a new student or parent to ask a question—provided that there is a staff person responsible for monitoring those questions and responding. This is something that is featured on the website for New Trier High School, which has two campuses—one for 9th graders in Northfield, Illinois, and another for grades 10–12 in Winnetka.[6] Questions submitted on the website are referred to a "transition coordinator." More about New Trier's transition planning and support procedures is featured in Chapter 9.

New Student Survey

Using school and district websites to link with new families can have mutual benefits—parents and students can find out about their new school, and school staff members can learn about their incoming students. That's what administrators at Naperville Central High School, outside Chicago, had in mind when they designed the "move-in survey."

The three-page survey was designed with the input of the counseling staff and teachers after officials noticed that a lot of the students who were in need of intervention services were those who were transitioning in during their high school years, says Pete Flaherty, a dean of students at the school.[7] The survey asks incoming students about topics such as extracurricular activities, attendance, whether they have had any honors classes, and even if they have previously used a combination lock. The information is then passed on to a counselor who will meet with the student once he or she arrives. The survey allows educators to plan in advance for the student's arrival in terms of assigning the student to a class and matching him or her with programs and services.

Social Media

As in the business world, having a website is not the only way to connect with potential "customers"—or families. Schools also should take advantage of Facebook, Twitter, Instagram, and the growing number of other social media tools available. Parents and children relocating to a new school may or may not use these apps to engage with school staff members or other students and parents. But a presence on these sites can help inform people about the culture of the school, the events that are taking place, and ways to get involved.

In his 2012 book, *Social Media for School Leaders: A Comprehensive Guide to Getting the Most Out of Facebook, Twitter and Other Essential Web Tools*, Brian J. Dixon says that using Facebook is an essential strategy for engaging a school community.[8]

"The old real estate adage is true: It's all about location, location, location," Dixon writes. "To communicate with students, parents and the local community, go where the people are. Facebook is the new town hall, the new civic center, the new hub of community activity—which is exactly where your school needs to be."

Once families are part of the school, social media can continue to be one of the vehicles they use to keep up with what is happening, converse with other parents and students, and develop a sense that they are part of the school community. It also continues to keep parents and students in touch with their friends after they have moved on to another school.

Compared to students who had to change schools before the advent of social media, today's students are able to continue to interact on a daily basis with their friends through Twitter, Instagram, Facebook, Snapchat, and other tools that seem to be popping up in the App Store every day.

There are certainly downsides to the importance that many students place on these sites, and both educators and parents should monitor students' use and reinforce proper digital etiquette and safety. But schools and parent organizations can support the positive, supportive, and appropriate role that social media can play in students' lives by creating school Facebook pages and using other platforms to keep current, former, and even future students and families connected. Social media can help a student feel as if he or she is not really saying goodbye and can be used to meet students at a future school. Both students and parents can post questions through social media that members of that online community can answer, and they may prefer doing this than calling the school office.

Deanna Creighton Cook, the community school coordinator at Manzano Mesa Elementary School in Albuquerque, New Mexico, increased her school's presence on Facebook and Twitter after a survey showed that parents weren't satisfied with the school's communication strategies, which mostly included paper newsletters and flyers.[9] She also created a separate page for the school's military families so they could "be a support system for each other." Parents use the Facebook page to post questions for each other, Cook said, adding that she also uses it to gather data on issues important to the school.

Paige, one of the students featured in Chapter 3, says she used Facebook to connect with one person whom she knew was attending her new school. "I had the ability to at least know one face and ask small questions here and there," she says.[10]

Text Messages

Both children and adults now largely depend on text messages and alerts on their mobile phones to remind them of scheduled events and stay in touch with friends and family members throughout the day. We receive texts to remind us of dentist appointments, to let us know when car repairs are done, and for a wide variety of other reasons. Because of the widespread use of mobile technology, education and community organizations are increasingly using texts to get their messages across to the population they are trying to serve.

For example, researchers at Stanford University created a text messaging program called Ready4K! in which parents of children attending preschool in the San Francisco area received weekly text messages with simple reminders on how to build their children's early literacy skills, such as pointing out rhyming words or saying words that start with the same letter sound. The researchers' study showed that the program increased the amount of time parents reported spending on early literacy activities in their home.[11]

As another example, in connection with the GEAR Up program, mentioned in Chapter 7, students in 14 West Virginia high schools received text messages providing reminders related to college planning and could, in return, text an actual college counselor with any questions they might have. Participants in the Txt 4 Success! pilot program received messages about tests they needed to take, when they could register for classes, and where they could find information on colleges.[12]

Districts, schools, and well-meaning program providers should be careful not to overwhelm incoming parents and students with too many messages regarding programs and services. And they should allow new families to opt in or out of receiving the messages. But both of these examples can inspire similar efforts to connect with and support new students and their parents in a way that is convenient for them.

A school's parent organization, for example, could send messages about upcoming meetings or events. And if a school has a peer-welcoming program, those student leaders can text a new student with a reminder to meet for lunch or try out a particular club, for example. In large high schools, where students may not cross paths every day, these messages can be very helpful and make the new student feel included. With proper planning, these messages could begin even before a family arrives in the district and can serve as another way to connect parents and students with people who can answer their questions.

Webinars

Educators use webinars for networking and professional development—why not to welcome new families? The content could include a simple greeting and some background about the school, ways for students and parents to get involved, special events held throughout the year, or how students can get extra help with classes if needed. Presenters could include the principal, a parent, a counselor, and even a student. As with an in-person orientation, time should be allowed for questions and answers.

A school's website and social media pages could be used to advertise the date of the webinar and how to participate. Parents who have already registered their children for school could also receive an email invitation to participate. Even if a child is already attending the school, parents would likely appreciate the opportunity to hear more information about the school and ask questions that they might not have thought about before their child was enrolled.

A webinar should be held at a time when most parents are not working, such as early evening, but the school could also save the presentation and supporting materials so a parent could view them later.

Live Streaming

On its website, Knapp Elementary in the North Penn School District live streams monthly PTO meetings, school assemblies, and other events to accommodate parents who can't attend in person.

"Not every parent can take time off from work to attend school day performances," says Gwen Pescatore, a parent leader at the school.[13] "This gives them the ability to watch from work. And recently, often extended family from places as far as India sign on to watch from afar. We do many things to help ensure families are part of conversations as early as possible." This is another strategy that can help incoming families get an idea of what is happening at the school and how they can participate.

Transfer Alert

School websites can also be used to alert parents to let teachers and administrators know if they will be moving again. Even if a school has procedures in place to support students who are changing schools, those strategies can't be helpful if the school doesn't know a child is leaving. The message could list how to request transcripts or other records, how to ask for a letter of recommendation from a teacher, or other documentation that can make the transition easier.

Conclusion

Connecting virtually with families is never a replacement for face-to-face interaction but is now equally as important. Reaching out through websites and social media demonstrates to parents that schools are considerate of their busy lives, which are likely even more hectic when moving is involved.

Connecting in Person

Even if a school or district has done a good job providing thorough information on its website or has made efforts to connect online with incoming families, that work might be in vain if the school doesn't feel inviting once the students and parents arrive.

As parents have shared, that first reception that families receive when they walk into a school or district office can determine whether they view the new school community as welcoming or unwelcoming. Schools—as well as individual teachers—should have procedures in place for when someone new walks in the door. For example, previous work on schools serving military children showed that many Department of Defense Education Activity (DoDEA) schools ask parents to wait a day after enrollment before their child starts class. This gives the teacher and the students in a class a chance to prepare for the new student. They get a desk, books, and other materials ready—thus allowing the new student to feel less as if he or she is a disruption. Clearly, DoDEA schools are accustomed to welcoming new students all the time, but it's a practice that could be implemented in any school.

This chapter focuses on how to make early face-to-face interactions with new students and parents a positive experience. Every new family in a school needs that person who can say, "If I don't know the answer, I will find out who does." The approaches described here not only create an initial welcoming atmosphere, but also provide families with links should they need more information.

District-Level Practices: Welcome Centers

Many school districts have a central location where families can receive information on the district and learn about the enrollment process, school choice options, community resources, and additional services. Welcome centers tend to be more common in a school district that handles registration at the central office level, instead of in each local school, and especially if the district serves an immigrant population.

In addition to providing information on registration, these centers often provide information on other community agencies and services that families might need, such as housing, food assistance, child care, and after-school programs. "We are a one-stop shop for families where people walk out feeling much better—more enriched, informed, and better prepared—than when they walked in," describes Marta Bentham, the ombudsman and director of family services for the Hartford public schools.[1] "We make sure that the Welcome Center is there for you to support the day-to-day living of your family, to help you assess your needs, and to answer your questions."

Think of taking a road trip and stopping at a welcome center in another state. Those sites employee friendly and helpful people who can answer questions and make visitors want to learn more about their state. School district welcome centers should have a similar effect on new families.

The examples that follow show how school districts are changing their procedures to improve parents' initial experiences with the on-site registration and enrollment process.

Temecula Valley Unified School District Welcome Center

Part of the *Welcoming Practices* Consortium, the Temecula Valley Unified School District (TVUSD), in Riverside County, California, handles registration of new students at its central office. When the district's new Welcome Center, as seen in Figure 5.1, opened in 2014, the staff in the registration office would send families who still needed to complete forms over to the center, which has computers for visitors, to finish the process. But that just added an extra step for parents who still had to return to the registration office to submit everything. So officials flipped the process to make it more convenient for incoming families.

"The Welcome Center is the first stop in enrollment," explains Diana Damon-White, the director of special programs for TVUSD.[2] "It allows us to catch parents that don't have their information prior to meeting with the enrollment techs." The staff can help make copies, send and receive faxes, and answer questions about district procedures—almost like a FedEx Office branch for parents (see Figure 5.1).

The center also provides welcome packets for military families and information on other resources in the community. The center was featured in an issue of the *Welcoming Practices* newsletter.[3]

Providence Public School Department Registration Office

All families enrolling in the Providence, Rhode Island, schools for the first time must come to the district's registration office to hand in documents, fill out forms, and complete the process. The office is plain and not necessarily inviting. Rows of plastic chairs fill the waiting room, a place where parents and children can sometimes spend long

FIGURE 5.1 Welcome center sign. Credit: Building Capacity/Welcoming Practices staff.

periods waiting, especially during peak times of the year. As with any waiting room, parents—especially if their children are with them—can get impatient or even angry if they don't have the right forms or if they don't understand something about the process.

In recent years, however, the district has been working with Ready to Learn Providence, an early-childhood education organization, to create a small reading and activity corner in the registration office to engage children and parents while they are waiting. Ready to Learn staff members were actually there to recruit parents for a parent education program, but they also helped answer questions about the registration process and helped parents fill out forms if they had low literacy skills in an effort to make the overall process more pleasant. See Box 5.1.

"It tells parents the schools care about them and want their involvement," Ready to Learn Providence director Leslie Gell said in a 2014 press conference.[4]

This is a practice that any district with a central registration location could borrow. Parent volunteers could help answer questions or read to young children if staff members were not available. Even if registration can be handled at a school office, creating a

---

BOX 5.1 "Creating Welcoming Places"

The Creating Welcoming Places Workbook from Community Activators, a consulting organization, walks members of organizations through a series of questions to determine whether their environment is inviting to people. The workbook lists several "milestones" schools can consider in determining whether they are making newcomers feel welcome.

Visit

http://www.abcdinstitute.org/docs/WelcomWorkbook_final%20copy(3)%20copy.pdf

small, child-friendly area with coloring materials and books can make a school seem a lot more inviting.

School-Level Practices

If a district does not have a welcome center—and even if it does—there are still many simple practices that local schools can use to create a welcoming environment for a new family. These are especially important if a family's first stop is the school their child will attend instead of a district location. New families entering a school should be made to feel special—not as if they are interrupting something.

Open House

Most independent schools begin the process of welcoming their new students and families—and their prospective new families—long before the school year begins. Many use an open house event to describe their school, its philosophy, and any unique features. This is not the type of open house that schools hold after the school year begins. These open house events are more like a recruiting strategy and bring together current families, members of the faculty, trustees, alumni, and others to present a picture of what it's like to be part of that school's community.

Administrators know that parents are essentially shopping for a school that best fits their child's needs so they are describing how they can meet those needs. In the competitive world of independent schools, these open house events are a way to market a school, but they also communicate a sense of belonging and welcome to families. These events offer families an opportunity to make early connections with other families as well as with teachers or school staff members who can answer questions they might have during the application or enrollment process.

Public schools, of course, often don't know which students and families will be part of their school until the first day or even after Labor Day. But holding a similar type of event can help a school stand apart from the crowd, in a sense, and gives families who do have a choice a clearer idea of their options. With the growth of charter schools, online schools, and other school choice options for parents, schools that want to create a welcoming environment for parents and children can hold an open house to help families connect with the school staff and with each other.

Welcome Tables

Welcome tables placed near the front door of a school are a visible way to demonstrate that school staff members are ready to greet anyone coming in and that they want to help those who have questions or concerns. Schools can place a table near the front door where a staff person, a volunteer, or even an older, responsible student can greet people who walk in the door and direct them to the office. As with the front door of a school, sometimes the school office is not easy to find.

Similar to a welcome center, a welcome table could provide information on registration, the parent association, after-school activities, or upcoming events. Some districts also prepare welcome kits or bags that include information on the district, maybe a few school supplies, and even coupons for local businesses. Schools can work with the business community to collect donations as well.

Tours

Offering to take a new student or family on a tour of the school campus not only helps them learn their way around but also gives them a chance to ask questions during the process. New parents and students are more likely to feel comfortable talking as they're walking around the building rather than standing at a reception desk while phones are ringing and other people are coming and going for various reasons. Staff members, parent volunteers, and older students can all be given the responsibility of giving school tours, perhaps with certain people being "on call" during scheduled weeks.

Classroom Visits

School administrators have become strict about not interrupting instruction during class and might be reluctant to let newcomers stop at classrooms while teachers are teaching. But offering to let an incoming student spend some time in a classroom of his or her grade level can allow the child to be an observer at first without immediately being expected to jump into what the class is doing. This practice can make the child's actual first day seem less unfamiliar. Arranging these visits ahead of time can avoid the issue of interrupting learning for other students.

Informing the Staff

Front office staff members can take some steps to let the school know a new student has enrolled. At a school in Lincoln, Nebraska, a new student's name and photo are emailed to all staff and faculty members in the building, giving them the chance to welcome the student when they meet him or her on the playground, in the hallway, or in the lunchroom.[5]

Portfolios

Sometimes new students bring a folder of work from their previous school—something either suggested by a teacher or a parent who wants to make sure the child makes a good impression on a new teacher. It's important that someone at the new school—whether it's a counselor or the child's new teacher—actually looks at the work and, ideally, uses it as a way to get to know the student and have a discussion about his or her goals, favorite subjects, and interests. The work itself might not be used to make decisions about placing students in appropriate classes, but it can certainly help form an important connection with a child.

Maps

Students serving military-connected children often hang up a large map near the front of the school that they use to pinpoint the variety of places where students have lived or where parents have been deployed (Figure 5.2). This same practice, however, could be used in a school without a lot of military families. When a student arrives—whether it's from a neighboring county or from another country—a pin or a dot could be added to the map to illustrate that students come from a variety of backgrounds. It's a small gesture that could make a family feel welcome.

Connecting Students and Families

Many of the questions and concerns on the minds of students transitioning between schools can best be addressed by other students who have been in the school for a while. Incoming parents can also benefit by having other parents to talk with about issues such as after-school activities, convenient places to buy supplies, or just other tips to help their children settle in to the new school.

Some students and parents might not need these connections for long, and they may even prefer to navigate the new system on their own. But what's important is that these connections and structures are available for those who need them.

"Regardless of when a child comes in the door, you have to have systems in place," says Stavem.[6] "This can't be a random event." She says that one reason she wrote her

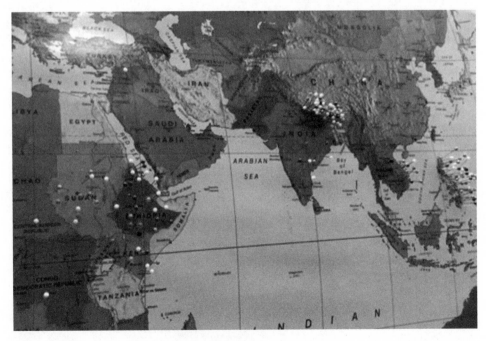

FIGURE 5.2 A map showing where students have lived.

book was because, as a principal, she noticed that while some teachers created a welcoming climate in their classroom, many were less than happy whenever she knocked on the door to introduce a new student. But that was because they weren't prepared for it, she says. Once teachers had a plan in their classrooms, she says she saw "a fundamental shift" in their attitudes toward helping a new student feel part of the group.

This section describes examples of different methods schools use to help new students and parents meet other students and parents. These can help families ease into their new environment much more quickly.

"Buddy Programs"

With peer "buddy" or mentoring programs, a new student is paired up with an existing student at the school who can help provide guidance during those first few days. The structure and duration of these programs obviously varies from school to school, but, in general, the welcoming students can serve as a bridge for newcomers—introducing them to other students, informing them of school rules and activities, eating lunch with them, and providing them with an inside view of social groups and opportunities to get involved.

Ideally, a school would have a system in place in which a student who enrolls in the middle of the year is connected with one of these mentors. Even if a school has such a buddy system in place, teachers can also make arrangements in their own classrooms for how students should welcome newcomers. If a school-wide buddy program is not in place, efforts by classroom teachers become even more important.

Laura Bradley, an English language arts teacher at Kenilworth Junior High in Petaluma, California, describes what she does when she is notified that a new student will be joining her class[7]:

"When our counselors notify us ahead of time (which they usually do), I try to be ready for the new student by figuring out a good seat," Bradley says. "Sometimes that means moving a couple students so that the new student is next to someone I think will be welcoming. I also keep extra get-to-know-you handouts from my first-week-of-school file on hand so that I have something for the new student to do in case the rest of the class is doing something that is difficult to jump in to."

Classroom teachers aren't the only ones who can think about how to pair new students with a buddy. Coaches, music directors, and even school food service managers can be involved in planning for how to make new students feel welcome and help them form positive relationships at their new school.

Echo Horizon School's "Host Families"

Located in Culver City, California, Echo Horizon School is an independent pre-K through 6th-grade school. The school's "host family" program is a long-standing practice used to welcome new families to the school.

Parents volunteer to host a family that will be entering the school in the fall. The strength of the concept is that both the incoming child and his or her parents have someone to connect with and discuss any questions that might arise during the transition process.

"We all felt that it was important to draw in the whole family, not just the child," says Paula Dashiell, who served as the school's principal for 27 years.[8]

Host families agree to meet their incoming family at a school gathering for all new families in the spring and then to organize some type of get-together over the summer before school starts. This can be at the host family's home or in a "neutral" location like a park or a casual restaurant.

The staff at the school takes care to match new families with those that have children of similar ages—such as a 1st-grade family hosting a kindergarten family. Once school starts, the host family continues to be a resource to the new family, answering questions about school policies and procedures and making sure they are aware of upcoming events.

"I think it's successful because it's easier to ask basic questions of enrolled families who had recently gone through the process rather than having to call the school and speak to me or find someone who may know an answer," adds Jenny Boone, who worked as the director of admissions and later as the school's assistant principal.[9]

Another family hosted Len and Susan Uhley when their daughter Olivia entered kindergarten at Echo Horizon. But they also turned around and became a host family years later. They found that they were also connected to the school's families outside of school through their work and the church they attended (Figure 5.3).

"Spending time with a host family can not only welcome you to a new school, but it can strengthen ties with the larger community," Ms. Uhley says.[10]

Since Echo Horizon is an independent school, families don't typically enroll during the middle of the school year, but the "host family" model is one that could be adapted for schools that do experience turnover during the year. Recruiting host families could be the responsibility of a parent association member. In schools with high mobility, parent leaders could also organize monthly newcomer gatherings if there weren't enough host families to match with each incoming family.

Student-to-Student

A signature program of the Military Child Education Coalition, Student-to-Student (S2S) trains both civilian and military students to develop and maintain programs to support students when they are moving between schools. There are actually three different versions of the program (Figure 5.4).[11]

- S2S: In the original program, high school students lead efforts to help incoming military students navigate their new surroundings and form positive relationships.

FIGURE 5.3 The Uhley family when Olivia started kindergarten. Credit: Uhley family.

FIGURE 5.4 S2S students learn games and activities they can try with club members at their schools. Credit: Building Capacity/Welcoming Practices staff.

- Junior S2S: This middle school version is customized to address the concerns of students in grades 6–8 and includes a focus on bullying prevention.
- Elementary S2S: This newer version for younger students involves more school professionals as supervisors and focuses on developing peer leadership skills among students.

The long-time use of S2S at a high school in Colorado has led to some successful practices that can serve as an example to other schools interested in using S2S or developing another type of student-led welcoming program.

Falcon High School is located outside Colorado Springs and serves military families based at the US Air Force Academy and three different installations—Fort Carson, Peterson Air Force Base, and Schriever Air Force Base. The school is also in a fast-growing area and receives between 200 and 300 new students, military and nonmilitary, throughout the course of the school year.

Counselor Greg Morris brought S2S to his school in 2006, when he met a student who had been eating lunch in the bathroom because she didn't have any friends to sit with in the cafeteria. The student then became involved in establishing S2S at the school. "She was a highly motivated young lady who didn't want others to feel the same way she did," Morris says.[12]

Morris receives about 200 applications each spring from students who want to be S2S members the following fall. His S2S leaders conduct the initial screening process and interviews and then Morris makes the final decisions, choosing 30 students.

To ensure sustainability of the program, he always makes sure his team has two juniors and two sophomores. This is recommended by MCEC for all S2S programs. At Falcon, the juniors take the lead and train the sophomores to be the leaders the following year. When the team members reach their senior year, they support the other welcoming activities led by the group. For example, when a new student enters the school, he or she is assigned to an S2S member. Then one of the seniors will also follow up with that student a few days later. "It's really exciting for an underclassman to be recognized by a senior," Morris says.

Morris adds that one of the most important lessons he has learned about recruiting S2S members is to look for students "with big hearts who want to help people." Many have also moved themselves and can easily empathize with a student who is going through a transition. At first, Morris says he made the mistake of choosing students based on their grade-point averages and teacher recommendations. But he says academically strong students don't necessarily make the best peer mentors. "Some high-achieving kids care a lot about themselves," he says, adding that if a student is only applying for S2S to add it to a resume, Morris drops that student from the list of finalists.

An activity called "mix it up" is one of the strategies the S2S members use to help new students feel less isolated at lunch (Figure 5.5). A member will go to a table and throw out a question or introduce a topic for a conversation that can include everyone at

FIGURE 5.5 S2S students lead a "mix it up" activity at lunch. Credit: Falcon High School.

the table. Sometimes it's about an event coming up at the school, and, in April, the topic is usually the Month of the Military Child.

The S2S students make sure new students know they can still join clubs even if they've enrolled after the beginning of the year, and they are taught how to check in periodically and identify whether new students are struggling and whether or not they are forming healthy relationships, Morris says. But he also notes that once it's clear that a new student has settled in, the S2S students know to back off.

Because the nearby middle and elementary schools don't have S2S programs, Falcon S2S students also go over to those schools to welcome and follow up with new students. Many of those students, he says are experiencing their first move and might need more time to adjust.

While each S2S program will develop its own procedures and activities, the program at Falcon serves as a good example on how to create a welcoming culture involving students who understand the challenges that come with changing schools.

Newcomers Clubs

Another method of helping students assimilate into their new school is a newcomers club. As with S2S, these groups can be organized by students who themselves were new in the past or who are interested in helping others. Participation in these groups might vary over time as students grow comfortable in their new school and no longer feel like newcomers, but they provide a sheltered environment in which new students don't feel alone and are able to ask questions about teachers, classes, or activities. Other models are organized by school social workers or counselors who can respond to any concerns students have and assist them in finding their place. Here are a few examples of how these types of clubs have been implemented:

- Students in an English to Speakers of Other Languages (ESOL) class at a north Georgia high school created a newcomers club where they could provide tutoring and support to newer immigrant students who are just beginning to learn English. A student who helped organize the daily group was inspired after seeing an ESOL student drop out of school. Teachers supported the student's idea and have set aside classroom space for the daily club session.[13]
- At San Onofre School in the Fallbrook Union Elementary School District in southern California, new students attend four group sessions in the newcomers club where they can talk about other places they've lived and schools they've attended.[14] At the end of the four sessions, they plant a flower in the school's "newcomers' garden," symbolizing a lasting connection to the school (Figure 5.6).
- Newcomers clubs aren't only for students. In the Edgemont School District in New York, a mother who moved to the community from Samoa began the club to help parents—many of whom come from overseas—connect with each other and learn from those who have been there a while. "The goal is always social," says Rebecca Webb, who helps organize the monthly "coffee mornings" and keeps the group's Facebook page updated.[15] Club activities continue to evolve, with a few members starting a band, some getting together to play golf, and others going into New York City to visit the United Nations or an art gallery. At the beginning of the year, they host a family barbecue and also invite school administrators to one of the coffee mornings so newcomers can ask questions and the district staff can learn about the concerns of parents. Webb says, "it was the simplicity of it" that has contributed to the club's success. "There's no obligation. We know it's tough moving to a new community. It's a place to chat, feel connected, and then go home." See Figure 5.7.
- At several schools, counselors will hold what they call a "lunch bunch" with new students in the school in which the students gather to eat, play games, and just get to know each other. Participating in a lunch group during the first few days or weeks in a new school can help to alleviate some of the anxiety new students face about where and who to sit with at lunch time. These gatherings also allow counselors to discern whether new students are handling the transition well or if ongoing support might be needed. A club could also be designed so that it involves a few students who went through a school transfer previously so they can talk about what helped them through the process. See Box 5.2.

FIGURE 5.6 A newcomer's garden. Credit: Carolina Miranda.

FIGURE 5.7 A gathering of Edgemont Newcomer's Club members. Credit: Edgemont Newcomer's Club.

BOX 5.2

Involving relatively new students in welcoming other newcomers can benefit both groups. Paige, from Chapter 2, explains.

"Being able to meet two other students and start this group is what gave me a chance to devote my sadness and anger toward moving into something. It changed to be a positive outcome and a way to make that high school truly mine and a place with a positive impact. Instead of dwelling on the 'new kid' status, I tried to eliminate this problem by helping install this wonderful program that helps new kids at school adjust to the pressures and negativity of moving. It definitely was the most influential part of my entire childhood and is the reason I am the person I am today."

Ambassadors

Another strategy is to identify volunteers to serve almost as neighborhood captains—or ambassadors—for incoming families. This idea is used at Oakridge Elementary School in Arlington, Virginia, and Principal Lolli Haws commented on the practice in an *Education World* column called "The Principal Files."[16] The names and contact information of these ambassadors are given to new families when they arrive. "That is a list of parents who are willing to be called by any other parent who has a question," she says. "Parents love the lists."

Ambassadors can also represent certain groups at the school, such as families of students with special needs or students in the gifted program. At the middle and high school levels, other groups could be represented, such as students in sports or performing arts.

Parent University

Districts across the country now offer a variety of free courses for parents that can help them become more involved in their children's education and informed about instructional issues and child development (Figure 5.8). In the Charlotte-Mecklenburg Schools in North Carolina, for example, courses in Parent University feature topics such as "Nutrition for the Early Years" and "Building Study Skills and Avoiding Homework Headaches."[17]

These types of programs offer another vehicle for helping new parents meet other parents who can answer their questions and help inform them regarding district and community programs. A class or mini-course could be created that is geared toward new parents in the district—sort of an orientation but with a lot of time for parents to socialize and get to know each other.

Another example, mentioned in Chapter 5, focuses not so much on parents who have moved into a new district, but more on parents who are transitioning to high school with their students. John Hancock College Preparatory High School, on the southwest

FIGURE 5.8 Parents attend a Chula Vista Elementary School District "parent academy." The session focused on ways to help students succeed in school. Credit: Building Capacity/Welcoming Practices staff.

side of Chicago, uses its Parent University program to welcome incoming 9th-grade parents and discuss how to support their children's education.[18] Once parents complete the program, they often take on leadership positions and help other new parents find ways to get involved in the school.

Welcoming Immigrant Families

Immigrant families arriving in the United States are no longer settling only in large urban areas. Most school districts across the country—urban, suburban, and rural—have seen their immigrant student population increase. Population studies show that more than 20% of students in US public schools have at least one foreign-born parent, and that figure is growing.

These statistics not only mean that numbers of English-language learners are increasing, but it also means that schools are sometimes welcoming children who have had very limited educational experiences in their own country. Families that are unfamiliar with the way schools operate need much more support than those who are just moving from one state to another. This section describes some examples of how school districts are accommodating the needs of immigrant students.

International Welcome Centers

The type of welcome center described earlier in this chapter might include bilingual parents or staff members on call if a non–English speaking family arrives to register or has other questions. But some districts that experience a large influx of students from other countries have created international welcome centers to specifically serve families who are new to the United States. These centers have translation services available, will help parents to complete documents, and will often assess students' English skills to determine where they should be placed.

Newcomer Classes

Students without any formal education likely won't be successful in a bilingual or English immersion class because they first need to learn what it's like to go to school. Some of these children might not have even learned to read and write in their own languages. Some districts have created newcomer classes as a temporary intervention where students can receive instruction targeted to their specific needs. These classes also allow students to form relationships with peers facing similar experiences as well as teachers or aides who can monitor how they are adjusting to school. Additional tutoring and enrichment opportunities can be offered on Saturdays or after school to support growth in literacy and math. See Box 5.3.

New Arrival Groups

Similar to clubs for military-connected students, which several schools in the *Building Capacity/Welcoming Practices* school districts have implemented, a new arrival group can provide a support system for students who have arrived from another country. Such a group might especially be helpful for refugee students or those who have had to leave family members behind. School psychologists, counselors, and social workers can play important roles in making schools welcoming instead of uncomfortable for these students. Chapter 9 provides some additional details about the importance of working with community partners when serving immigrant families.

Interventions for At-Risk Students

Some programs and interventions have been developed for particular groups of students who are more likely to experience difficulties with transitions. For instance, many schools have transition programs in high schools to help students with disabilities move either to college or to employment in the community. Other programs target at-risk students or those in foster care.

Hyoun Kim and Leslie Leve, scientists at the Oregon Social Learning Center, developed the Middle School Success intervention to prevent and reduce substance use and delinquency in the transition to middle school. "Given that substance use and other co-occurring problem behaviors tend to increase substantially during middle school years, preventive interventions for preadolescent girls aimed at reducing risk for a set of problems are urgently needed," Kim said in an interview.[19] She added that although middle school can be a difficult transition for many, it is an ideal time to provide effective interventions for girls in foster care.

BOX 5.3 Supporting Immigrant Students

A 2012 report from the Center for Applied Linguistics identified successful characteristics of programs for newcomers:

- Flexible scheduling of courses and students
- Careful staffing plus targeted professional development
- Basic literacy development materials for adolescents and reading interventions adapted for English-language learners
- Content area instruction to fill gaps in educational backgrounds
- Extended time for instruction and support (e.g., after school, Saturday, and summer programs)
- Connections with families and social services
- Diagnostics and monitoring of student data
- Transition measures to ease newcomers into the regular school programs or beyond high school

Visit

http://www.cal.org/resource-center/publications/helping-newcomer-students

---

In their review of evidence-based interventions to support students with disabilities in their transition to 9th-grade high school, Loujeania Williams Bost and Julia Wilkins of the National Dropout Prevention Center for Students with Disabilities identified practices that are especially effective.[20] These include:

- Pairing current high school students with incoming freshmen as peer mentors
- Holding a freshman class orientation while students are in middle school
- Offering summer programs at the high school to increase students' academic skills, orient them to the layout of the school, and enable them to meet high school teachers
- Providing tutoring for students who are unprepared for rigorous academic work.
- Personalizing the learning environment through small class sizes, a freshman academy, mentoring programs, or student participation in school activities

Additional examples of successful transition programs for middle and high school students are featured in Chapter 7.

Conclusion

This chapter highlighted just some of the creative strategies schools are using to help new students and their parents meet other families and find answers to the many questions that can arise when entering a new and sometimes confusing environment. Schools can use these ideas or adapt them to fit the needs of their own school communities.

6

Welcoming Younger Students

There has been a growing movement over the past decade or more to make a child's entrance into kindergarten less of an abrupt experience. Transition programs and prekindergarten-to-3rd grade efforts across the country focus on bridging the gaps between what children experience before kindergarten and the routines and expectations of elementary school. These initiatives range from bringing greater alignment between preschool curriculum, teaching practices, and assessment to giving young children ample opportunities to visit kindergarten classrooms and experience the learning environment before school starts.

Even if a child has attended preschool, moving into an elementary school can feel intimidating for a 5-year-old. The hallways are bigger, the other children in the school are bigger, and there are many more adults involved in the whole process (Figure 6.1).

Relationships among schools and the child care centers, preschools, and other community organizations that interact with parents who have young children can lead to more opportunities for young children to feel less anxiety about starting school. Several organizations, including the National Association of Elementary School Principals[1] and the Massachusetts-based Community Advocates for Young Children,[2] provide training and guidance to principals on adapting their schools to serve younger children. The W. K. Kellogg Foundation[3] has also made large investments across the country aimed at creating stronger links between schools and the early-childhood community.

Many of these efforts also target families whose children have not been in any formal early learning program because these children often lack the early academic and social-emotional skills needed to do well in today's more academically focused kindergarten classrooms. Schools of education can better prepare future teachers and administrators by including training on young children's development and on strategies for supporting their transition into school.

FIGURE 6.1 Welcoming a young student. Credit: Laura Fuhr, *Fairfield Citizen*.

Children with disabilities and their parents may experience additional stress in transitioning into school. Rules and regulations regarding eligibility requirements, services provided, and community resources can be confusing and are not always readily available to parents. A tool such as the WelConnect app mentioned in Chapter 4 may be an effective and convenient way to help families that are interacting with a variety of agencies and providers.

The issue of welcoming children into kindergarten is complex and can fill a book on its own, and, indeed, there are many existing resources on making schools more inviting to young learners. This chapter highlights some models that are being implemented across the country.

It's also important to note that even schools that work hard to make new kindergarten families feel welcome might not be giving the same attention to students who enter school at other times during the year or at other points in their education. Teachers and school leaders could possibly adapt practices geared toward young children to fit the needs of older elementary-level students who are transitioning between schools. Home visits by teachers, summer transition programs, and other practices could be implemented in schools with high mobility as a way to make the transition experience less stressful.

Ready Freddy

The University of Pittsburgh's Office of Child Development created the Ready Freddy transition model in partnership with the Pittsburgh public schools to address the problem that too many 5-year-olds were enrolling late to kindergarten, after the school year started. The program is designed to involve the entire family in the transition process. A transition team was created that ultimately developed the Ready Freddy[4] model—a series of activities for children and parents that include school transition teams, summer kindergarten clubs targeted to at-risk families, and a frog mascot to help raise awareness about the importance of on-time enrollment.[5] Schools using the model, for example, place frog footprints in the hallway to direct newcomers from the door to the school office. They make sure there are sufficient visitor parking spaces, and they provide materials to parents on preparing their children for kindergarten.

Lessons from Ready Freddy that can be applied more broadly and for older students include posting signs and directions so new students can more easily find their way around the school campus. In fact, sometimes not even the main entrance of a school is easy to find, so posting signs outside the school can also keep new families from feeling lost.

Well-labeled maps of the school—similar to a store directory in a shopping mall— could be placed throughout the school. New students tend to not want to stand out as new students, and knowing their way around is one way to avoid that.

Another lesson is conducting some type of community outreach to locate new families and opening school buildings during the summer for tours or incoming student "clubs."

Home Visits

Schools have sometimes conducted home visits when a child is chronically absent or when there are other causes for concern. But these visits are increasingly being used to help establish relationships between teachers and new students before the school year begins.

Organizations in 18 states are now affiliated with the Parent Teacher Home Visit Project, which is based in Sacramento, California, and provides resources and training opportunities regarding home visits by teachers.[6] Some schools conduct these visits every year—not just to welcome new kindergarten families.

With young children, however, the visits are a way to break down barriers between home and school. Highland Elementary School in the Gresham-Barlow School District, for example, is one of several schools in Multnomah County, Oregon, that has been implementing this practice.[7] The visits are simple and don't last long. The teachers just drop by to say hello and leave a postcard if no one is home. But Kammy Beyer, a kindergarten teacher at Highland, says the effort helps make the statement to families that "we're in this together."

"For the parents, we always ask them and expect them to come to school," she says. "I think it's important to say, 'Hey, I'm willing to come to you.'"

Research is also showing that home visits can benefit both teachers and families. A study on the Kindergarten Home Visit Project in Durham, North Carolina found that teachers who conducted home visits were more likely than those who didn't to report wanting to reach out to disengaged families and gaining a better understanding of the diverse needs of families. And non–English speaking parents who were visited reported feeling more comfortable in the school.

In the study, 44 teachers and 928 families from 19 elementary schools were randomly assigned to participate in home visits or not. The researcher, Amy Schulting, from the Center for Child and Family Policy at Duke University, wrote that the visits were conducted with an emphasis on gaining the parent's perspective on his or her child.[8]

"In typical home–school communication programs, information is frequently communicated to parents about their children's performance or ways to support academic achievement at home. Less frequent is the opportunity for parents to share their expertise regarding their own children with educators," Schulting wrote in a newsletter article for the Family Involvement Network of Educators, a community of educators, researchers, and others organized by the Harvard Family Research Project. She added that the home visits "gave parents the opportunity to talk to and feel heard by their children's teachers, right in their own homes. It also helped parents and teachers build a positive and trusting home–school relationship at the very beginning of the school year."

Home visits also give families an opportunity to ask questions or share information that they might not feel comfortable sharing or get the chance to at busy drop-off and pick-up times or during parent gatherings at school.

Summer Transition Programs

Many school districts schedule summer transition programs for incoming kindergarteners as a way to introduce young children—especially those who have not been in preschool—to the classroom routine and to get a jump on early literacy and math skills. These programs can range from a week to several weeks, depending on how they are funded and whether facilities and a staff are available to run the program.

Teachers say they are able to address many of the social adjustment issues during these early weeks, allowing them to focus on teaching once school starts. Studies have found that children do acquire kindergarten-level skills during these programs, and, anecdotally, teachers report that sometimes children are mastering standards that wouldn't even be taught until later in the fall.

Since 2010, a growing number of school districts in Multnomah County, Oregon, have been offering the Early Kindergarten Transition (EKT) program, which includes

FIGURE 6.2 An early kindergarten transition classroom. Credit: SUN Community Schools.

transition activities for both children and parents. An initiative of the Schools Uniting Neighborhoods (SUN) community school system, in partnership with the school districts, EKT is now in place in more than 30 schools in the county (Figure 6.2).

Andrew Mashburn, a professor of developmental psychology at Portland State University, has been evaluating EKT to gather best practices and information on the various ways the program is being implemented. His 2014 report provides a summary of practices schools are using to ease students' transition, such as arranging classrooms exactly as they would be during the school year and giving children opportunities to familiarize themselves with all areas of the school and become acquainted with other school staff members.[9]

Lessons from EKT can also help inform other efforts to welcome younger students into new schools.

Staggered Starts

The first few days of kindergarten can be an overwhelming experience for 5-year-olds—and for their parents.[10] So, to minimize the stress involved, some schools stagger the beginning days for students. This can be handled in different ways. For example, at Highland Elementary mentioned earlier, kindergarten teachers organize classes of incoming students into smaller groups of about seven children. Each group then attends school for just one day during the first week of school while their parents join the school's principal and counselor for a welcoming meeting.

Since there are only about seven children in each group, the practice allows teachers to give the students more individual attention on their first day as they learn school and classroom procedures. Teachers also use the time to give the state's kindergarten assessment and get a feel for the skills of the students.

Older Buddies

Many schools foster their older students' emerging leadership skills by pairing them up with incoming students in kindergarten or pre-K. The buddies can read to the younger students, work on projects, organize games at recess, or provide support in other ways. These programs can help young children quickly feel attached to their new school and are a good model for how to welcome new students, regardless of their age. Other examples of buddy programs will be discussed at other points in this book.

Student Snapshots

Children with special needs are much more than a label. That's the idea behind the "Student Snapshot" practice developed by the Pacer Center.[11] The Snapshot is a one-page information sheet that parents can use to introduce their child to his or her new teachers and other school personnel who might interact with the child. The Center recommends keeping the information simple and personal, including a photo and sharing information on the child's strengths and challenges and likes and dislikes. Schools could also promote this simple activity and even help parents prepare the personal statement, further creating a more welcoming environment for a transitioning student with a disability.

Conclusion

These various strategies are strong examples of what schools can do to relieve the anxiety that has in the past been associated with starting kindergarten. Teachers, school leaders, and families can work together in similar ways to make changing schools less of a disruption for a child academically, socially, and emotionally. Many of these strategies can also be adapted for an older elementary student who is new to a school.

Welcoming Older Students

While some practices typically used with young children—such as summer transition programs and home visits—can be adapted to accommodate older students, there are also strategies that specifically address the questions and concerns of middle and high school students and their parents. Often faced for the first time with multiple classes, these students are trying to find their place and adjust to new expectations in several classrooms, not just one. These campuses are also typically much larger, so students need additional time to learn their way around—one tour might not be enough.

Even for students who aren't moving to a new community, the transition into a middle or high school can be a stressful and uncertain time. So having a plan for providing extra support for students who are changing schools during these years can prevent students from struggling and feeling isolated.

The Search Institute, a Minneapolis-based research organization, has identified 40 developmental assets that researchers say adolescents need to develop into healthy, caring, and responsible young adults.[1] They are organized into external and internal assets. External assets include conditions such as positive family communication, providing service to others, and having positive adult role models. Internal assets refer to qualities such as being motivated to achieve, reading for pleasure, and having the skills to resist negative peer pressure.

Educators working with students who are changing schools during their middle and high school years can consider ways to foster these assets when creating welcoming and transition-related programs and practices. Student leaders who assist in these programs, such as peer mentors and buddies, can also become familiar with these assets—to strengthen their own skills and to benefit students they are trying to support.

A variety of strategies exist for welcoming new students who are transitioning during a time when they might be trying to figure out what interests them, what kind of friends they want, and how to solve problems without help from their parents. Some of the programs mentioned here are not specifically "welcoming" or transition programs, but they include features that can help provide the additional support that mobile students might need to stay motivated and moving forward.

Orientation

Most schools provide some type of orientation for rising middle and high school students. These opportunities for students to preview their next school can range from a couple hours to a full day and can give students a chance to ask questions—often away from their parents—of staff and other students.

But shouldn't a student who enrolls in a school after the beginning of the year also get an orientation? While it might not be possible to devote an entire day to introducing new students to their school, a staff member and some student leaders could organize an abbreviated version of the orientation agenda for students who have entered the school within the past month or the past few weeks. Another strategy is to have a video orientation for new students to watch before they start school. The video could describe a typical school day, extracurricular programs at the school, how to buy lunch, who to talk to if there is a scheduling problem, and what to do if they can't open their locker or have another issue they don't know how to resolve.

Placement Tests

When students transfer, their official academic records often don't arrive at the same time. Placement tests, therefore, can help counselors and administrators determine the best classes for a student—especially at the high school level.

Naperville Central High School, outside Chicago, began giving transfer students two placement tests—one in reading and one in math—after administrators noticed that students were too often being placed in classes that were not a good fit. An "honors" English class at one school, for example, might not be as rigorous as one at another school and regular sophomore English might be a better fit, explains Pete Flaherty, a dean of students at the school.[2]

Using the assessments to make informed decisions about classes has also helped avoid the problem of a new student being placed in a class and then having to change again a week or so later because it was above or below his or her level. Schedule changes, he says, can make the transition process even more stressful.

Parents and students might interpret having to take a placement test as a sign that the school doesn't trust what they are saying about the child's academic ability. Parents might also be concerned that asking the student to take a test just after changing schools might create even more anxiety. So, this is an area where educators should be sensitive and inform families well before they enroll that the tests will be part of the process. Emphasizing the hope of placing the student in the most appropriate class and avoiding a schedule change could make the tests seem less of a burden.

Advisory Programs

Advisory programs, similar to a homeroom, are more common in independent middle and high schools, but many public schools also implement them to give students the feeling of a smaller community at a time when they are adjusting to being in a larger school.[3]

"Advisory programs have the potential to ensure that every child has a meaningful relationship with an adult and belongs to a community of peers," wrote the authors of a 2009 article in the *Middle School Journal*. "These elements of connectedness have the potential to improve academic achievement and the overall school experience for middle grades students."

The article also outlined the characteristics of effective advisory programs and advisors:

- Strong advisory programs address issues of community.
- Strong advisories promote open communication.
- Strong advisors know and care about their advisees.
- Strong advisors closely supervise their advisees' academic progress.
- Strong advisors are problem-solvers and advice-givers.
- Students and advisors perceive that advisory directly improves academic performance.
- Students and advisors perceive that advisory functions as a community of learners.

Some schools have taken other routes to creating advisory-type programs. A middle school in the Gwinnett County Public Schools, outside Atlanta, created some lunch clubs designed around different interests of both teachers and students. One club, popular with boys, focused on pathways to playing sports in college, for example.

The clubs brought together students with similar interests while also giving them another adult who would be able to notice if anything was troubling the student or if there were changes in behavior.

Gear Up

Gaining Early Awareness and Readiness for Undergraduate Programs (GEAR UP) is a competitive grant program of the US Department of Education that provides low-income and minority students with college awareness activities and support services, such as tutoring and mentoring. Schools work in partnership with higher education institutions and community partners to implement the grant. Because GEAR UP begins with a cohort of students in middle school—generally in 7th grade—and follows them through high school, there is special attention placed on students' transition from one level to the next.

A toolkit from Oregon GEAR UP, for example, describes a variety of strategies for addressing "four components of effective transition systems."[4] Those components are:

- providing students and families with accurate and useful information
- supporting students' "social success"
- preparing them for academic success
- collaborating to monitor transition plans

The GEAR UP model also includes the strategies of using "near peers"—high school students and recent high school graduates—to support younger students through tutoring, college visits, summer programs, and other supportive activities. While these efforts are focused on building "college knowledge," they can also help incoming students make connections with students who can answer questions and provide friendship.

Summer "Bridge" Programs

Similar to the summer transition programs for incoming kindergartners, many high schools have implemented similar "bridge" programs for rising 9th graders to make the larger environment feel less intimidating, help them get to know their teachers, and get a sense of a daily high school routine. Many schools, because of limited funding, target these programs for students who might be at-risk of not being successful in 9th grade. But if the school is already open and serving students, a segment of the program could be added for students who are new to the school, even if they're not entering 9th grade. These students could also benefit from a chance to learn their way around the building, meet other students, and find out about school activities. It's likely that this strategy might make the first day of class feel less confusing for a child who is new to the school.

Link Crew and WEB

Link Crew is a high school transition program in which upperclassmen are trained to welcome incoming freshmen and model appropriate behavior. The Link Crew team of students is involved in the orientation process. They do classroom visits throughout the year focusing on character development and academic success. They connect with freshmen through out-of-school social events and follow up on a more individual basis as well. The Link Crew leaders help to pass the school's culture on to the freshmen, focusing on topics such as the "in" dances, popular cheers at football games, and other aspects of attending their particular school.

WEB—which stands for Where Everybody Belongs—is built on the same foundation as Link Crew but has a curriculum that is more appropriate to younger adolescents. Eighth graders are trained to welcome incoming 6th or 7th graders, depending on the configuration of the school.

FIGURE 7.1 Link Crew leaders create a theme for their school tours. The theme for this group was Skittles. Credit: The Boomerang Project.

More than 4,000 schools in the United States and Canada have had staff members trained and certified by the Boomerang Project, which designed both programs.[5] And the number of schools participating grows every year, according to Micah Jacobson, one of the founders of the programs. Figures 7.1 and 7.2 show activities led by Link Crew members. Box 7.1 lists the three needs that students have when they are making a transition to a new school, according to the Boomerang Project.

The implementation of both Link Crew and WEB varies based on the personalities and needs of each school, but both programs are intended to support incoming students throughout the entire school year—not just during the first couple of days. And while the programs mostly focus on welcoming students at the beginning of middle or high school, students who enter in the middle of the year—or at 10th grade instead of 9th, for example—would also be connected to a Link Crew or WEB leader.

While Link Crew and WEB focus primarily on transition, schools that have implemented the programs report less bullying, improvements in attendance, gains in academic scores, and drops in suspensions and discipline referrals.

Don't Forget About the Parents

Just because teenagers are beginning to show more independence—even in the process of changing schools—doesn't mean their parents are out of the picture. Schools can

FIGURE 7.2 Students participate in a Link Crew group activity called 64 Squares. Credit: The Boomerang Project.

continue to provide information and opportunities to get to know other parents, but these activities can take place separate from their children. In Chicago, for example, John Hancock College Preparatory High School uses its Parent University program to help parents of rising 9th graders learn how to understand student data and advocate for

---

BOX 7.1 Transition Needs

According to the Boomerang Project, students have three fundamental needs when they are transitioning to a new school:

- Safety: Protection from bullying, rumors, isolation, and harassment
- Information: Focusing on issues such as what classes to take, where those classes are, what rules are important, what opportunities are available, and where they have to be when
- Connection: This is more likely to happen when a caring, older student provides friendship and leadership

their children.[6] Workshops are held simultaneously with the school's "freshman connection" program, allowing parents to participate in a parallel transition program.

Community Connections and Resources

Again, it's important to consider that some students are receiving services in the community and may be connected to other professionals, such as foster care caseworkers, mental health providers, or military school liaison officers. It's important for schools to work with these providers so that services can continue and so educators can learn more about the particular needs of these transitioning students. In addition, schools that receive many students with special needs may want to consider collaborating on grants to help transitioning students. This is another example where school personnel could use the WelConnect app, or a similar service, to locate resources in the community.

Conclusion

At the elementary level, parents are actively involved in their children's transition into new schools—they're largely asking the questions and often taking steps to ensure that their children are making friends. But at the middle school level, and certainly in high school, students start to navigate new schools on their own. Transition and welcoming programs for older students should be informed by research on young adolescents and incorporate practices that encourage positive development.

8

Lessons from Business

As noted in the Hanover Research report mentioned in Chapter 3, an increase in competition among schools has led to many administrators thinking more about students and parents as customers—and not simply as people who are required by certain geographical boundaries to attend a particular school.

As a result, some educators have turned to companies that are known for outstanding customer service in order to improve the culture of their schools. Others have found inspiration in the work of Stephen Covey[1] or other experts on leadership and effective business practices.

In the Tulsa Public Schools, for example, leaders recognized inconsistencies in how people were treated when they went into a school's front office, which can sometimes become like what one district official described as a "three-ring circus." They've since taken several approaches to improving how secretaries and other office staff members in the district receive new parents and students.[2]

"When we enroll a child in our schools, we're engaging with the whole family," says Jane Barnes, the director of staff development and leadership training for the district. Some schools have received training from local Chick-fil-A and QuikTrip franchises in Tulsa. And now the district is providing additional professional development to school office staff members on how to be more attentive to families who walk in the door and leave a "positive, memorable impression."

Barnes says receptionists and other office employees need opportunities to practice various scenarios in which they interact with families. The training also focuses on strengthening the collegial relationships among those working in a school office and improving their skills in communicating with Hispanic families.

Other districts across the country have taken lessons from "the happiest place on earth" on how to make schools more inviting and improve relationships with families. In a piece for Forbes.com, contributor Carmine Gallo wrote about how Disney employees have a way of making everyone feel that they are special.[3]

"Disney employees are trained to be 'Assertively Friendly.' Disney team members are encouraged to actively seek contact with guests," he wrote. "For example, they will approach an individual who appears confused instead of waiting to be asked for directions. When I was at Disneyland with my wife and two girls, an employee noticed we were trying to figure out who would take the picture. 'I'd be glad to take the picture for you,' he said. That's assertively friendly."

It's not hard to imagine how such training could be applied in a school setting, with office staff members who can anticipate parents' questions and are eager to minimize their confusion.

Disney Institute, located in Lake Buena Vista, Florida, is the professional development division of the Walt Disney Company. The institute provides workshops to a variety of organizations, including school districts, on how to create systems in which employees deliver outstanding service. The Montgomery County Public Schools in Maryland, the Broward County Schools in Florida, and the Elizabeth Public Schools in New Jersey are just a few of the hundreds of districts that have participated in Disney training (Figure 8.1).

FIGURE 8.1 Disney also helps student leaders learn how to implement welcoming practices in their schools. These Oceanside, California, high school students participated in Disney's Approach to Leadership and Teamwork program, part of the Disney Youth Education Series provided for students at both the Florida and California parks. The students learned "ice-breaker" activities they can use to help welcome new students to their school. Credit: Building Capacity/Welcoming Practices staff.

In a 2012 blog post for Catapult Learning, an educational services company, Susan Abelein, a senior advisor, wrote that "nearly every aspect of Disney's business practices can be applied to educational institutions, from how district offices are run, to individual school buildings, to individual classrooms. The notions of service theme (mission), cast (employees), setting (environment), and process (operations) may be integrated and applied. As the new school year commences, one particular aspect is worth analyzing, and perhaps even reimagining and reforming. That aspect is Disney's approach to guest service as it relates to our school parents. First, who are our guests? Quite simply, our guests are every single person that enters the school building; they are stakeholders, community members, parents, students, etc. For our purposes, school parents are used as the primary example of our guests."

Lessons from Industry Leaders

Whether schools look to Disney, Chick-fil-A, Starbucks, Nordstrom, or another company for inspiration, leading companies provide some lessons for future administrators and teachers on how to provide excellent service and create satisfied "customers."

Hiring the Right People

When asked how Nordstrom trains its employees, one of the founders of the company is known for saying "We don't train them. Their parents train them." When it comes to hiring staff members who will be among the first to greet new families, it might be just as important to hire secretaries and receptionists who are service-oriented as it is to hire those who have computer and record-keeping skills.

Many local school advisory committees, which include parents and community members, now have input into hiring principals. It may be that those committees should also review candidates for office and registration-related positions.

Creating Consistency

A comment often made about Starbucks is that its products and services are consistent—a grande latte served at a shop in Manhattan is unlikely to differ from one served in Los Angeles. Applying that same principle to schools, the process of registering a child in a district shouldn't vary from school to school.

In the Tulsa district, for example, one issue that contributed to confusion and frustration for new families was that office staff members at a school would tell a parent that they didn't have the necessary documents to enroll. But then the parent would go to the district office and be told something different. The office staff members "didn't feel supported" by the administration, says Marsha Owen, who trains support staff members in the district, and then parents would view that office employee as someone who was creating an obstacle for them.

The requirements for registration should be clearly posted on a district's website and schools should follow those procedures. If gas or electric bills are required as proof of residency—but not water or phone bills—those kinds of details should be provided in a checklist. Schools within a receiving district should also not be inconsistent in how they approach enrolling students who have been receiving special education services in a previous school. Even though the Individuals with Disabilities Education Act requires districts to provide the same level of services outlined in a child's Individual Education Program (IEP), schools will sometimes want to conduct their own tests before making decisions about providing special education. Such a delay, however, can mean that a student is not receiving the support he or she needs. In 2013, the US Department of Education sent a letter to state special education directors to make this point.[4] Even if services for the student might change once a new evaluation is conducted, the school is still obligated to follow the previous IEP until those decisions are reached.

Parents and students in the midst of changing schools shouldn't hear something different every time they walk into a school or district office. Making sure enrollment procedures are clearly communicated to the staff people who are likely to be answering questions is part of creating a welcoming environment.

What might vary from school to school, however, are the extra steps used to integrate new students and families into the community. One school might have a morning coffee break for new parents. Another might provide a school tote bag with some welcoming gifts such as coupons and maps, and a third might schedule individual meetings with a counselor for new students and parents. Those are the types of practices that will reflect the unique personality of each school.

Extra Touches

A lot of people can take documents from parents and enter information into a computer to register students into a school. But not everyone will have paper and crayons on hand for a young child who has to wait in an office or offer to take a family that has dropped in unexpectedly on a tour of the school, or remember a new student's name if he or she comes into the office with a question.

Successful businesses are known for going beyond the level of service that is expected of them. Chick-fil-A, for example, is often held up as an example of this because their employees provide services that are not typical of most fast-food restaurants, such as bringing orders to a customer's table, asking them if they would like refills on their drinks, and even having umbrellas to walk customers to their cars in the rain. It's what the company refers to as "second-mile service."

Creating an Atmosphere

Even in a crowded, hectic shopping mall, there is something relaxing about walking into a Nordstrom store. Sometimes a pianist is playing soothing music, there's a coffee shop attached to the store, and the furniture placed throughout the departments is comfortable. Walking into a school shouldn't raise parents' stress level; it should lower it and create a sense that they've found the right place.

Schools can create happier reception and waiting areas with comfortable furniture, fresh flowers for a table, children's artwork on the walls, and even pleasant background music. Parents, students, and community members can lead these kinds of projects.

At the Culver Family Learning Center, part of the Evansville-Vanderburgh School Corporation in Indiana, for example, a local florist donates fresh flowers to place on cafeteria tables every morning. Staff members at Duryea Elementary School in Houston make a point to shake hands with students and parents as they walk into the building every morning. Many other schools involve students in creating and maintaining school gardens to help beautify the campus. These kinds of projects not only make school buildings more inviting, but they are also a great way for new students and families to get involved (Figure 8.2).

FIGURE 8.2 Fresh flowers daily. Credit: Culver Family Learning Center.

Conclusion

There are some limitations to applying business principles to schools. But it's clear that lessons can be learned about how to make someone who is uncomfortable feel comfortable or to help clear things up for someone who appears confused. Meeting newcomers' needs helps to build a rapport with those students and parents. They will remember the staff members and others who took the extra time to make them feel welcome.

The Role of Staff and Community Partners

One reason that student transition between schools hasn't received the attention that it should is because schools traditionally have not had staff members directly in charge of assuring that welcoming and transition procedures are in place. Monitoring how students are adjusting to their new classes, routines, and peer groups can fall by the wayside until a problem arises.

"Nobody owns that piece," says Robin Harwick, a Seattle University researcher who previously worked at Treehouse, a nonprofit agency that provides educational services for children in foster care.[1] Too often, she adds, educators don't recognize that high mobility can negatively impact a student until behavior or academic issues surface.

But Micah Jacobson, of the Boomerang Project, says that picture is beginning to change and schools are increasingly placing a counselor or other staff member in charge of transition-related activities.

A variety of options are available to district leaders and school administrators who want to make sure that their schools are welcoming and that consistent practices focused on ensuring smooth transitions are being implemented. The following sections discuss some approaches that districts can explore to make sure someone is consistently attending to the needs of students and families in transition (Figure 9.1).

Transition Teams

One of the best ways to ensure that teachers and other staff members begin to think about how they can create more welcoming environments is to create a team that focuses on the topic. Jacobson notes that creating a team increases the likelihood that programs will be sustained when there is staff turnover.

FIGURE 9.1 In her role as a project specialist with the Oceanside Unified School District, Margaret Malek (*right*) works with the S2S teams to welcome new students. Here, she participates in an activity at a training session. Credit: Building Capacity/Welcoming Practices staff.

The North Carolina Department of Public Instruction has created a detailed transition planning guide that outlines steps for smooth transition from preschool through college and outlines some of the topics that can be addressed by a district-wide transition plan.[2] These include planning professional development on the issue of transition, reviewing research-based practices, addressing issues of alignment as students move through grades, seeking input from families on their transition experiences, and recruiting volunteers to help with transition-related gatherings. At the district level, these teams could include representation from an enrollment planning office, student support services, curriculum and instruction, a parent leader, a community member, and even a student. School-level teams can also be formed to focus on implementing welcoming practices at the local level. Having a team keeps the work from falling on one person and can raise awareness about the issues that students face when they are new to a school.

While guides such as these tend to focus on transition experiences for students who are progressing through schools in the same district, they can also help educators think about the type of support needed for students who are moving in and out of the district.

Teacher Leaders

Teachers are increasingly looking for hybrid roles and leadership opportunities in their schools as a way to advance in their profession—without having to leave the classroom.

These roles can include coaching and mentoring other teachers or serving as technology specialists. Taking charge of creating welcoming procedures, organizing a club for newcomers, or leading a transition team can be one of these roles. For an example, read the profile of New Trier High School in Chapter 10.

Parent Liaisons

Schools receiving Title I funds to serve students from low-income homes sometimes have parent liaisons who serve as a resource for parents, answer questions, and often organize workshops or other parent activities. In some cases, they also take an active role in creating welcoming environments for new students and families. Nicole Webb (Figure 9.2) worked as a parent liaison with Fallbrook Union High School, near the Marine Corps Base at Camp Pendleton. In her role, she worked with students to create Helping Hands, the school's version of MCEC's Student-to-Student (S2S). In addition to welcoming new students, the club members also organize community service projects.[3]

In the Temecula Valley Unified School District, a family engagement specialist was hired to operate the Welcome Center, described in Chapter 5. In that role, the specialist helps newcomers complete the registration process and participates in community events that involve the district.

FIGURE 9.2 Nicole Webb served as parent liaison for Fallbrook Union High School. Credit: Building Capacity/Welcoming Practices staff.

Flexible Funding and Staffing

Giving schools with high mobility the flexibility—and funding—to assign staff members to focus on students in transition is another approach. In the Gwinnett County Public Schools, a large suburban district outside of Atlanta, there is a long-standing practice in which additional "staffing points" are allotted to schools with high mobility.[4] The higher a school's mobility rate, the more points a school earns to hire part- or full-time employees. Schools in which at least 30% of the students qualify for free or reduced-price lunch also receive some additional points—regardless of their mobility rate—since there tends to be a relationship between poverty and student mobility, explains Sidney Camp, the district's executive director for human resources staffing. These schools might not qualify for Title I but, under this formula, would still qualify for additional points.

"One size does not fit all," Camp says. "As long as we have variation in where kids come from, in what kinds of schools they've been enrolled in before, and what their language skills are, we've got to make sure our schools are able to provide additional support to serve those students."

Having enough staff members to promptly handle students' records is one reason for the additional positions, but these funds could also be used to support welcoming activities, gatherings for new families, or other efforts to help in the transition process.

Community Partners

Outside agencies and community partners—especially colleges and universities—are a valuable resource for providing additional support for students who might need some extra attention if they are struggling after changing schools. Below are a couple examples of partnerships that have been formed between schools and other organizations that can provide support to students going through a transition.

Partners at Learning

Partners at Learning (PAL) is a long-running service-learning program at the University of California San Diego (UCSD) in which undergraduates provide underserved students with one-on-one tutoring and support.[5] The college students earn course credits and gain valuable experience, especially if they are considering working in education or in another field serving children and youth (Figure 9.3).

In partnership with USC's *Building Capacity* consortium, a focus on children from military families was added to the program so that the college students would understand the challenges faced by those students. The *Building Capacity* team was interested in connecting PAL with consortium schools because military students are sometimes in need of academic assistance due to frequent school changes. UCSD is also in an ideal position to focus on the needs of military families since it is located in a region with

FIGURE 9.3 A PAL tutoring session. Credit: Building Capacity/Welcoming Practices staff.

several military installations. The partnership demonstrated how university students can help meet the needs of students in a particular community.

Adopt-a-Class

Founded by a businessman in Cincinnati, Adopt-a-Class[6] is a mentoring experience for businesses and civic groups. The mentors who adopt a classroom of students are much more than business partners. They visit their adopted classrooms as a group, become pen pals with students, plan activities, and provide not only academic support, but also focus on students' communication skills and enrichment. Businesses that participate report that adopting a class is a positive team-building experience for their employees, and teachers say the program helps improve students' attendance and writing skills.

The program is a model that could be adapted to focus on schools with high mobility or on creating practices to welcome new families to a school.

Culturally Specific Agencies

As mentioned earlier, schools are serving an increasing number of immigrant students and families. These families are often unfamiliar not only with the US education system, but also with the communities in which they are living. Schools that form relationships with cultural organizations that are helping to settle immigrants and refugees can improve the way they communicate with and support families that are new to the United States. The staff at these agencies can inform school staff members where resources are available to immigrants and refugees and perhaps whether there are particular practices or gestures that might be offensive to certain ethnic and cultural groups.

In Multnomah County, Oregon, for example, schools have long partnered with the Immigrant and Refugee Community Organization (IRCO) to support families from Africa and Asia that are moving into Portland Public Schools and surrounding districts.[7] IRCO provides funds for after-school and early-learning programs as well as other services to improve outcomes among the children and families they serve.

These kinds of partnerships can help schools by bringing in those who have the expertise to work with immigrant families, and they help the families by making the schools seem less unfamiliar and confusing.

Resource Fairs

Communities often host resource fairs or other events in which organizations can set up a booth and offer information about the services they provide. Schools and school districts can use these family-focused gatherings to connect with new families in the area. In one of the *Welcoming Practices* districts, for example, an organization named the Chula Vista Community Collaborative held an event called the Day of the Child, focusing on health and wellness. Schools participated and demonstrated the WelConnect app (Figure 9.4).

Professional Development

Creating school and district practices that are sensitive to students' transitions takes some planning and some work. While knowledge on the effects of student mobility

FIGURE 9.4 Staff members from the Chula Vista Elementary School District participate in a community event. Credit: Building Capacity/Welcoming Practices staff.

FIGURE 9.5 A training workshop on transition. Credit: Building Capacity/Welcoming Practices staff.

should become part of teacher and administrator preparation programs, those already working in schools should receive some training on the variety of strategies that are available.

Organizations such as the Military Child Education Coalition offer training sessions on supporting students in transition. But district personnel, such as those who work with students in foster care or in school social work, for example, could also share some knowledge that would benefit any student who has changed schools. As discussed in the previous chapter, businesses that focus on customer service might also offer tips that could be adapted for a school setting (Figure 9.5).

Conclusion

No one really disagrees that a school should be a welcoming place but because of the multiple demands on teachers and school staff, the needs of students and families in transition are sometimes overlooked. It's important to have structures in place so staff members or volunteers know their roles in keeping the needs of new families at the forefront. In addition, schools don't have to address the needs of mobile students on their own. There are also examples of partnerships between schools and neighborhood associations, mental health agencies, and youth development organizations in which extra support is made available to students who are falling behind or need some additional attention.

The Importance of Following Up

The transition period for a child into a new school lasts much longer than the initial visit and the first few days. And, even if a school made sincere attempts to welcome the child, introduce him or her to peers, and make sure the student was comfortable in the new surroundings, those gestures may "wear off" after a while.

That's why it's important to develop a system for checking in with those students who have changed schools for reasons other than the typical moves from elementary to middle or middle to high school. A few indicators can help demonstrate whether a student has adjusted well to his or her new community or still feels disconnected or out of step with other students—grades, attendance, participation in extracurricular activities, and behavior. In this chapter, some different strategies schools are using to monitor how students are transitioning and address concerns or gaps in a student's progress are also highlighted.

As mentioned earlier, the needs of students who experienced a proactive move may be quite different from those of students who left a prior school because they or their parents were reacting to something.

Grades

How is the student performing? Is homework being turned in on time? If the student's grades are lower than they were in his or her previous school, it's possible that he or she has missed some critical pieces of the content being taught. Review district and community-based options for getting the student some tutoring or additional instruction to fill in those learning gaps.

Attendance

Students who change schools in the middle of the year sometimes miss days because of a move. This can lead to a drop in performance, as noted in Chapter 1. If the child continues to miss days, the problem will likely get worse. Missing too many days of school can be an indicator that the child is struggling with the transition and hasn't made the connections to students and adults that are necessary to develop a sense of belonging.

Several school districts in recent years have increased efforts to improve attendance rates and to communicate the problems associated with chronic absenteeism. Attendance Works, a national initiative, has been working with districts across the country to address the issue in their communities and features several case studies on its website. Its 2014 report, "Absences Add Up: How School Attendance Influences Student Success," shows how poor attendance affects children from the early grades through the high school years.[1] Focusing on data from the National Assessment of Educational Progress (NAEP), the study shows a connection between absenteeism and lower performance on the NAEP.

"This is true at every age, in every racial and ethnic group and in every state and city examined. In many cases, the students with more absences have skill levels one to two years below their peers. While students from low-income families are more likely to be chronically absent, the ill effects of missing too much school hold true for all socioeconomic groups."

Attendance Works also recently released a toolkit called the Power of Positive Connections that suggests strategies for improving attendance among at-risk students, such as using data to determine which students need additional support and creating a team of school staff members and community partners to implement strategies for increasing attendance.[2] As with assigning buddies to walk incoming students through the first few days in a new school, schools can create an "attendance buddy" program so a new student has additional encouragement to come to school every day, if needed.

Tardiness

Students might not be missing school, but what if they are chronically late? When families move, their home lives can remain in disarray for some time. Getting organized for school each day might be one of the areas that is suffering during the transition.

As students get older, there might be more complex reasons why they are late. They might not feel connected to other students yet and are trying to avoid before-school social situations.

Schools, however, can help encourage on-time attendance by raising awareness of why it's important and creating incentives. The Perfectly Punctual Campaign, developed by LearnLead and now part of Attendance Works, provides materials that schools can use to get both children and parents involved in getting to school on time.[3]

In higher grades, some schools have instituted what they call "bell-ringer" activities or questions that students can tackle during the first few minutes of class and use to earn extra credit. Whether schools use rewards for being on time or consequences such as detention, this is another area where data can help educators understand whether mobile students are more likely to be tardy than others.

Extracurricular Activities

Involvement in extracurricular activities at school, such as sports, performing arts, or clubs, is one indicator that a student has settled into his new school and is beginning to make connections with those who have similar interests. A student who is not pursuing interests outside of class might feel isolated, which could lead to negative behavior and outcomes.

Past research has found that students who participate in some type of extracurricular activity are less likely to get in trouble in school and are more likely to have higher grade point averages and complete high school.[4] "The positive effects that extracurricular activities have on students are behavior, better grades, school completion, positive aspects to become successful adults, and a social aspect," Erin Massoni, of the College of DuPage, wrote in a 2011 paper.

Counselors' and teachers' initial conversations with new students can focus not only on their academic strengths and needs but also on what they enjoyed in their previous school or neighborhood and what they want to continue doing or try for the first time. Personally introducing students and parents to those in charge of the activities that interest them—instead of just giving them a name and a number—can also make it easier for the student to follow through with getting involved. Schools can also create procedures that make it easy for students to jump into a program in the middle of the year instead of placing too many restrictions on when students sign up.

It's important to note, however, that involvement in positive activities doesn't necessarily have to take place at school. Participation in programs provided by community groups and local sports organizations can also mean that the student has weathered the transition successfully and is pursuing something he or she enjoys. Sometimes highly mobile students would prefer to pursue interests or build relationships with peers outside of school because this might make moving again easier.

Behavior

If new students are having a hard time following school rules, it might be important to ask whether the rules were clearly communicated to them. Having buddies and peer mentors share basic information about what is and isn't allowed at a particular school is one way to help new students adjust and might seem less overwhelming than being told to read a student handbook.

If students who recently transitioned are getting into trouble at school, there could be multiple reasons—one of which might be that they are reacting to being picked on or are trying to stand up to students who are being bullies.

A study by the *Building Capacity* research team at USC showed that students who have changed schools multiple times—four or more—are more likely to carry weapons to school and experience victimization by other students.[5] This includes physical victimization, such as being pushed or shoved and having property stolen, as well as nonphysical incidents, such as being the subject of rumors and being made fun of because of one's looks.

The study, which looked at outcomes among both military-connected and nonmilitary students, found that the rates of victimization and weapon-carrying were higher among military-connected students who had experienced repeated deployments of a family member. The study reinforces the point that changing schools is often just one transition that a student is experiencing, so it's important for educators to be aware of other changes that are happening in a student's life around the same time. Below are some examples of how schools are monitoring students' progress over time. Boxes 10.2 and 10.3 provide additional examples.

Strategies for Following Up and Addressing Concerns

Check and Connect

Check and Connect[6] is a system for following-up with and mentoring students who are considered at risk of disengaging from school or dropping out. Designed by researchers at the University of Minnesota, the intervention has been used for more than 25 years in schools across the country and internationally. Mentors are trained to recognize the warning signs that students might be losing interest in school and then serve in almost a coaching role to keep students motivated. The checking refers to regularly monitoring data on issues such as grades, behavior, and attendance. The connecting aspect refers to implementing interventions that are specifically designed to meet students' needs and working in partnership with the family. The program is also designed to provide long-term support—up to two years—for students.

A student who has recently changed schools might be doing fine academically and showing no signs of being "at risk." But the Check and Connect system provides an infrastructure through which a new student—or one who has changed schools multiple times—can at least be temporarily assigned to a Check and Connect mentor.

Studies show that schools using the model see decreases in truancy, tardiness, behavior referrals, and dropout rates and increases in attendance, credits earned, and graduation rates. Cindy Marten, superintendent of the San Diego Unified School District lists Check and Connect as one reason that the district had the lowest dropout rate among California's large school districts, according to a 2014 report by the California Department of Education.[7]

Check and Connect has identified three primary options for staffing the program—each of which has pros and cons. One option is to hire dedicated mentors, another is to appoint existing staff members as mentors, and a third is to partner with community volunteers to serve as mentors. Depending on the model used—especially if it is implemented district-wide—mentors can also "follow" a student who transfers to another school.

Naperville High's "Red Card"

When students reach middle and high school, it can be more challenging to determine how well they are adjusting to all of their classes. Naperville High School, mentioned earlier, developed a system for collecting feedback on students when one or more teachers begins to notice behaviors that could indicate a student is falling behind or struggling in other areas. The "red card," named for a school color, is a simple one-page document (Figure 10.1) that can provide a more complete picture of a student and is often used with students who have recently transferred into the school, Flaherty says.

Once one teacher or staff person makes a referral, the form is then sent around to all of the student's teachers to collect information on academic, behavioral, social-emotional, and other issues that teachers might be seeing. These might include:

- Poor organizational skills
- Problems completing homework
- Drug concerns
- Being confrontational or disrespectful
- Crying or moodiness
- Excessive tardiness
- Falling asleep in class
- Frequent bathroom visits

Meetings with the student, parents, and other staff members—as well as the interventions recommended—are also documented, producing a record of how the school is responding. Schools may have similar procedures in place for when it's clear that students are getting off track or having discipline issues. But establishing a practice in which teachers are collectively reviewing how new students are doing in all of their classes could be a more proactive way to support those who have recently changed schools.

Playworks (and Other Strategies for Improving Recess)

Recess, like lunch, can be an awkward time of the school day for new students. They might not be invited to join games, they might not know the inside jokes that students are laughing at, and other students might even pick on them.

In recent years, however, schools have been increasing their efforts to provide more structure during recess time in order to reduce conflict while still giving students the physical activity and time for free play that they need (see Box 10.1).[8]

Playworks is a nonprofit organization that trains school staff members to create positive experiences for students during recess.[9] A direct-service model of the program

RED CARD

Student Name: **ID:**   **Date of Referral:**

Staff Name: **Class Subject:**

CONCERNS (check all that apply)

Academic:

- ☐ *failing/near failing*
- ☐ *homework completion*
- ☐ *test-taking skills*
- ☐ *poor organizational skills*
- ☐ *unprepared*
- ☐ *lack of focus*
- ☐ *appears unmotivated*
- ☐ *possible misplacement*
- ☐ *other:*

Behavioral:

- ☐ *disruptive*
- ☐ *confrontational/disrespectful*
- ☐ *bullying*
- ☐ *hyperactive*
- ☐ *change in peer group*
- ☐ *drug concerns*
- ☐ *inappropriate references related to sex*
- ☐ *inappropriate references related to gangs*
- ☐ *other:*

Social/Emotional:

- ☐ *family issues*
- ☐ *crying*
- ☐ *moody*
- ☐ *withdrawn*
- ☐ *anxious*
- ☐ *inappropriate social interactions*
- ☐ *verbal/written reference to suicide (personally deliver to SPS)*
- ☐ *other:*

Attendance:

- ☐ *excessively tardy*
- ☐ *excessively truant*
- ☐ *excessively absent – excused*
- ☐ *requests to leave the room frequently*
- ☐ *other:*

Medical:

- ☐ *frequent health office visits*
- ☐ *sleeps in class*
- ☐ *frequent bathroom visits*
- ☐ *significant weight change*
- ☐ *poor personal hygiene/unkempt appearance*
- ☐ *frequent evidence of injuries*
- ☐ *other:*

INTERVENTIONS TO DATE (check all that apply)

Discussed Issue with:

- ☐ *Student: # of times:*   *Approximate Date(s):*
- ☐ *Parent: # of times:*   *Approximate Date(s):*
- ☐ *Student Service's staff: Who:*   *Date:*
- ☐ *Other*   *Date:*

Accommodations offered (Please mark if it was accepted or rejected by student):

- *Accepted* ☐ *Rejected* ☐ *Change seat/work group*
- *Accepted* ☐ *Rejected* ☐ *Test / quiz retake; # of times:*
- *Accepted* ☐ *Rejected* ☐ *Draft of work turn in before due*
- *Accepted* ☐ *Rejected* ☐ *Test review w/ teach; X#'s:*
- *Accepted* ☐ *Rejected* ☐ *Redbook checks*
- *Accepted* ☐ *Rejected* ☐ *Other*

Recommended:

- ☐ *A.M. Math Support (room 343); Dates:*
- ☐ *A.M. Chemistry Support (room 323); Dates:*
- ☐ *A.M. Writing Center (room 245); Dates:*
- ☐ *Academic Center (Math, Com. Arts. Science, Humanities, Periods 4,5,6, Room 117); Dates:*
- ☐ *After School Studies Skills Academy (Tues & Weds, 3:30 – 4:30, Room 117); # of times*
- ☐ *Other*

Please email any additional comments when returning this form

FIGURE 10.1 Red Card.

BOX 10.1 "Friendship Room"

"The one thing I did like at that site is that they had a friendship room. Recess can be a very difficult time for students, especially new students, and this option was a great one for my children to do activities and meet new people."

— *Parent's response to survey about transition*

provides schools with a full-time coach to help oversee recess activities, make sure students have plenty of options and play equipment to choose from, and intervene if conflicts arise between students.

The model also includes a junior coach program in which students are trained to be peer leaders on the playground. A 2012 study by Mathematica Policy Research and researchers at Stanford University showed that "investing in recess and organized play can prevent bullying, improve students' behavior at recess and readiness for class, and provide more time for teaching and learning."

Some schools are implementing strategies similar to those used at Playworks schools. At Santa Margarita Elementary School—located on Marine Corps Base Camp Pendleton—former principal Pat Kurtz worked with her playground "duty supervisors" to make recess time less stressful and empower both the students and the supervisors to create more positive experiences for students.

When she would bring a child into her office because of a behavior problem, she would also have the duty supervisor, who likely intervened in the situation on the playground, be part of the conversation so he or she could learn from how Kurtz worked with a child who is struggling with peers. Her goal was to show these employees "how you can interact with a child in a positive way that is going to foster their growth instead of punishing them."

This practice also began to send students a message that these staff members are part of the school's leadership and have authority.

Through the Peaceful Playgrounds program—which focuses on how to make the best use of recess time and space—the supervisors have been encouraged to have as much playground equipment and games available as possible to avoid situations where students are competing for limited supplies.[10] Santa Margarita is a "school full of sergeants' kids," Kurtz laughs. "They all want to be the leader."

She also worked to foster relationships between the duty supervisors and students. If a student is having a particularly tough time, he or she is assigned a "duty buddy" who checks in with the student throughout the day for as long as it takes the student to connect with other students in a more positive way.

Another strategy has been to have students play before they eat lunch. If conflicts arise, they are more eager to resolve them so they can go eat. Kurtz and her staff, however, didn't just create a new atmosphere for students on the playground. They also made use of a room just off the playground that has been more suitable for some students having problems with social interaction.

Instead of putting students back in the same situation where they were struggling or bullying other kids, they can retreat to the Lunch Recess Options (LRO) room, which is filled with computers, games, art supplies, Legos, and other materials that students can use if the playground is a troublesome place for them that day. Some students also

BOX 10.2 Attendance Review Team

In this summary, Attendance Works highlighted the Chula Vista Elementary School District, another *Building Capacity/Welcoming Practices* district, for the way it monitors students' attendance and addresses repeated absences.

Well before the rest of the nation had even heard of the term "chronic absence," Chula Vista was measuring it and addressing it, thanks to a forward-thinking district administrator. As a result, the mid-sized city, just seven miles north of the Mexican border, has seen more than a decade of sustained attention and efforts to reduce chronic absence in its schools.

The results have been encouraging: only 4% of students in grades K–3 in the 2010–11 school year were chronically absent. The community has interventions in place so that when students miss too much school, principals work with those students, their teachers, and parents to resolve the problem. Strategies include meeting with parents, conducting School Attendance Review Team (SART) meetings, counseling students, referring to community resources, and recognizing improved attendance.

Names of students who exceed the district threshold for excused or unexcused absences are provided to principals quarterly. This report ranks every school in the district in terms of attendance, using data from the previous three years. Recognizing that they cannot do their jobs if the students are not in school, administrators use this information to communicate with parents and to monitor the effectiveness of their truancy intervention programs.

Families who need help can turn to any of the five Family Resource Centers operated by the Chula Vista Community Collaborative and located in the district, which offer a range of services to any family needing additional support. Once a school has exhausted its resources, the principal refers the student to the district's School Attendance Review Board (SARB). Initially developed to deal with truancy, SARB includes representatives from community agencies that offer family and student support. Each case is dealt with individually based on student data and family circumstances. Often the family is given a contract outlining expectations. The family is then invited to talk about progress.

If attendance does not improve, SARB can move forward with legal actions, such as a referral to Juvenile Court. Judges provide recommendations and expectations for parents to elicit positive changes in attendance patterns, advocating in the best interest of the children's future. Because of the many interventions in place, the school district has a low percentage of students with chronic absence. Still, several schools have chronic absence rates above 10%. Future plans include:

- Providing schools with daily attendance reports through a new Data Dashboard
- Creating an iPad application for students to track their own attendance
- Emphasizing the importance of good attendance as part of preschool and kindergarten orientations

Source: Attendance Works; visit
http://www.attendanceworks.org

BOX 10.3 New Trier High School
A System of Support for Transition

When the staff at New Trier High School realized that 8th-graders and their parents were experiencing a lot of anxiety as they prepared for the transition into high school, they decided they should create a structure to better support students coming from the six different suburban Chicago K-8 school districts that feed into New Trier. And they put someone in charge of implementing the plan for helping new families find answers to their questions and navigate the high school experience.[11]

Sue Ellen Haak, a health and PE teacher, was released from part of her teaching duties and given the role of transition coordinator. For her, the process of welcoming the next class of freshmen to New Trier starts when those students are still new to 8th grade. She visits all of the junior high schools in the fall to meet with the 8th-grade teachers and discuss any changes in the curriculum and the process students will use to select courses in 9th grade.

She first meets with students at all of the schools in the winter of their 8th-grade year to answer their questions, and then she returns in the spring as they are getting closer to finishing junior high. Another feature that sets New Trier apart from most high schools these days is its advisory program, similar to a homeroom. When freshmen enter the school, they are assigned to an advisory—a teacher and a group of 25 students that they will stay with for their entire four years of high school. Advisories meet for 25 minutes every morning of the school week. "That is kind of their home base," Haak says. "It's kind of their little family. The advisor system creates a situation where students get a lot of individual attention."

Student leaders from the senior class are assigned as helpers to meet with advisories a few times a week and support freshmen through the transition process. Advisors are also the main point of contact if a teacher begins to notice that a student is struggling in a certain area or having behavior issues. "The advisor holds the big picture of the child," Haak says. Some faculty members also serve as advisor chairs and will send a feedback form to all of a student's teachers if an issue appears to be more serious.

While the transition and advisory system was created with local 8th-graders in mind, it also works to support students who are new to the community or who enter the school during the middle of the year. If an incoming 9th-grader did not attend a local junior high—and didn't have the benefit of Haak's visits to the schools—he or she will meet with Haak for at least an hour, have a chance to ask questions, take a placement test, and then be assigned to an advisory. If a student enters the school after the school year has started, an assistant principal meets with the family and describes course options and other features of the school. The student will also take a placement test. Haak says the enrollment process actually takes about a week—much longer than families actually expect—because of the attention given to placing the student in the right courses and advisory. "We do try to make sure we have the right spot for them," she says.

New Trier High also has an annual "freshman adventure" program during the summer for students who have struggled in middle school or who feel the need to make a fresh start in high school. The program includes a day of team-building exercises and a camping trip so students can begin to develop friendships even before school starts. Because New Trier is a large high school with more than 4,000 students, incoming freshmen may rarely see their friends from 8th grade. Advisory parties are also scheduled at the beginning of the school year so the groups can begin to get to know each other. Senior helpers also attend and take everyone on a tour of the campus.

The infrastructure that the school has created to focus on transition also extends to training for school staff. Teachers working on administrative certificates, for example, are often assigned to work with Haak to help implement the transition-related activities.

Haak says she's never seen another school with a position that is similar to hers. Districts, she says, have to make a commitment to devote time and money to developing such a system.

use the room, which is supervised, to complete homework. Certain students also receive priority to use that room because it has been recommended by their teachers or by the school's special education teacher. Such a room, however, can also be used as a comfortable, less intimidating spot for new students who are still trying to find their place in a new school.

Learning Together

Learning Together[12] is a peer-tutoring program in reading and math that trains students to tutor struggling peers who are two grade levels below them. Implementation of the program is flexible, meaning it can be used during the school day, after school, or during the summer. The students who are selected to be peer tutors are not necessarily high-achieving students. In fact, they are often performing below the proficient level and might even have behavior problems at school. The purpose of the peer-tutoring match is to improve the performance of both groups of students, but especially the older tutors.

Learning Together is not designed specifically for mobile students, but it can be a good strategy for addressing any gaps in learning and for getting new students connected to their school. The leaders of one of the *Building Capacity* districts, Fallbrook Union Elementary School District, felt it was a good match for children in military families. A total of 230 students were placed in the program—with 6th graders tutoring 4th graders in Math Together and 8th–6th and 7th–5th pairs in Get Ready 4 Algebra. A profile of the district's implementation of the program on Learning Together's website provides this brief summary: "Preliminary results indicate tutors and tutees in both programs showed positive behavioral changes and significant academic improvements. Coordinators observed increased personal empowerment and self-efficacy for tutors and tutees; tutors not only assumed more responsibility for their own learning, but also for that of their tutees. Participants developed trusting, one-to-one relationships that benefitted the whole school climate." See Box 10.2 and Box 10.3 for more examples.

Preparing for the Next Move

School transitions sometimes happen with little time for the family or the teachers to prepare. A teacher might walk into the classroom one morning to find that a student withdrew the previous afternoon and there was no opportunity to say goodbye or tell the child that he or she will be missed.

These situations should not keep teachers or counselors from contacting the family and offering support through the process of transferring to a new school. If the child is relocating to another school in the district, a process can be created for teachers from the sending and receiving schools to communicate about the student if any questions arise—perhaps informally through an email or more formally by filling out a form.

If the district has a transition team, as described in Chapter 9, these individuals can make suggestions and create procedures to follow when a student transfers within a district. For example, a teacher or counselor at the sending school might fill out a form that accompanies the student's academic records and gives more descriptive information about the child's strengths, needs, and interests. Or a checklist could be created for families to remind them what documents and other information they should gather if their child is changing schools. The Military Child Education Coalition created such a checklist for military families, which could be used as a guide.[1]

If a teacher or other school staff member is aware in advance that a child is transferring—whether it's within the district or across the country—a variety of strategies are available for helping the family prepare for the change.

Exit Interviews

A discussion with the child and family before a move is a chance for everyone involved to review the student's academic progress and address any important issues that might need attention when the child moves into a new school. Similar to a parent–teacher conference, these meetings can help answer "what next" questions for both the parents and the child. If the child is making the transition before middle or high school, such an interview is a great time to help the child consider what classes or electives he or she might want to take in future years. An article that appeared on Military.com provides more in-depth suggestions on how to structure such an interview.[2] If the family is considering moving out of the attendance zone because of financial troubles, such a meeting might also be used to refer the parents to agencies or programs that can help them. It's possible that a move can be avoided.

Transition Liaison

The McKinney-Vento Homeless Education Assistance Act established a liaison program to make sure homeless students are identified and are receiving the services they need to be successful in school even if they have to change schools. Schools experiencing high mobility can learn from that model and assign someone to serve as a point of contact for families who are moving within the same district or to a nearby district—similar to Sue Ellen Haak's position at New Trier High, described earlier. Multiple districts in a metropolitan area could also contribute funding for the position to reduce the burden on one system. This liaison would be aware of enrollment policies and procedures for districts within the region and could direct families to the appropriate departments and to people in a district who can answer their questions. Districts could make sure that families are aware of this person's role before they change schools. Some metro areas have several districts, and a position such as this could help families avoid "getting the run-around" or being misinformed when they are transferring.

Records

The process of requesting student records in case of a transfer should be clearly posted in the school office or on the district website. Parents should be made well aware of these procedures, even if they never intend on moving. This helps them be more prepared in case a child does transfer, since it might take a few days for office staff members to respond to the request.

Schools often require "official" student transcripts and other documents to be transferred from a school office—not hand-carried by the parents. But schools should provide families with a copy of their file when they leave the school. It's possible that the receiving school will review the unofficial documents while waiting for the official records.

Saying Goodbye

As with welcoming a new student, there is no specific right way to send a student off to a new school. But it's important to show the student that he or she was valued and appreciated while at that school. These gestures and practices can build a student's confidence and help him or her through the next transition.

A Memory Book

With enough advance notice, teachers can involve their class in creating a memory book for a student who is leaving. A simple scrapbook will do, but with so many easy, inexpensive photo book websites, something more professional can also be created. Here are a few ideas for how students can contribute to the book, depending on their age:

- Draw a picture for the child who is leaving or write a short note saying something nice to the child.
- Include photos from the school year, highlighting special events, projects, field trips, performances, or class parties.
- Have students share their home and email addresses.
- Have children write a short poem for the child who is leaving.

Many of those same photo websites also offer other products such as mouse pads, t-shirts, pillows, and key chains. These items can also be used to create customized gifts for the child who is leaving. Teaching Success provides a list of other ideas.[3]

An Inspiring Book

Why not wish the transitioning child well and encourage reading at the same time? Giving the child a book that either talks specifically about changing schools or on facing new challenges in general is a great way to show the child that the school cares and wants to provide support through the transition. Here are a few suggestions:

- *A New House* by Jill Wenzel and Jan Westberg: "An activity book for 4- to 10-year-olds featuring puzzles, games, and activities that address the process of and emotions surrounding buying and moving to a new home."
- *Who Will Be My Friends?* by Syd Hoff: An easy I Can Read book about a character named Freddy searching for new friends after he moves.
- *My Name Is Maria Isabel* by Alma Flor Ada and K. Dyble Thompson: A book for ages 7 to 10 that focuses not only on a young girl's adjustment to a new school but also her desire to stay true to her family's heritage.
- *New Kid, New Scene: A Guide to Moving and Switching Schools* by Debbie Glasser, PhD, and Emily Schenck: A nonfiction guide for ages 8 to 13.
- *Tangerine* by Edward Bloor: An inspiring young adult novel about a legally blind boy who discovers truths about himself and his family after a move to Florida.

See Box 11.1 for another book-related idea.

BOX 11.1 Book Fair Idea

Lots of schools hold book fairs once or twice a year. A school that experiences a lot of mobility could dedicate a display table to books about transitions, meeting new friends, and adjusting to changes.

T-Shirts or Stuffed Animals

Both younger and older students would appreciate a T-shirt signed by their classmates and teachers. They might never actually wear it, but it will be something that has a lot of meaning to them in the future. A stuffed animal, such as a school mascot, is also an appropriate gift for a younger child who is moving away.

Portfolios, Again

As mentioned in Chapter 5, sometimes new students carry a folder of work or a favorite project to their next school—sort of as a way to nonverbally introduce themselves to teachers at their next school. In preparation for a move, teachers can help students prepare such a portfolio. This process can help remind students of their strengths at a time when they might be unsure of themselves.

A Special Note

Teachers or other staff members who know the student well—such as coaches, secretaries, or counselors—can write a short note expressing support for the child at this time of change and uncertainty.

Social Media

Most schools—and many individual classrooms—now have Facebook and other social media accounts with which to share information, photos, and videos related to student activities and accomplishments. Even after a student moves, these sites allow him or her to keep up with friends and teachers from the previous school.

Conclusion

Teachers may not always be able to check up on a student after he or she leaves for another school. But presenting the student with a gift or some other remembrance will help the child feel that he or she can stay connected to friends even after moving to a new school and community.

Conclusion

Each school's transition story is different, and it's important for educators to understand where their students are moving from, why they're moving, and if they're about to move again. Having a sense of these characteristics can help teachers, administrators, and other school professionals decide which practices are the best fit for their individual school.

While some routines and strategies can be implemented at the district level, such as opening a welcome center, creating an app, or having a standard registration process, the practices and environment at each individual school will make the most difference in whether children and families feel that they have been greeted with warmth and understanding.

Established transition programs tend to focus on students who are moving between levels, such as from elementary to middle and from middle to high school. These programs do offer lessons that can be implemented more broadly for students who change schools at other times as well. But great ideas on how to welcome, connect with, and support new families are also emerging from schools every day. Gathering and sharing these locally developed ideas can help contribute to greater awareness of how changing schools impacts students and to a collection of promising practices from which educators can choose.

Resources

This section provides links to a variety of articles and resources about creating welcoming practices in schools.

Welcoming Strategies for Newly Arrived Students and Their Families,
http://smhp.psych.ucla.edu/pdfdocs/practicenotes/welcomingstrategies.pdf

What Schools Can Do to Welcome and Meet the Needs of All Students and Families,
http://smhp.psych.ucla.edu/welcomeguide.htm

Findings from Evaluations of the Implementation of Multnomah County's Early Kindergarten Transition Program,
http://health.oregonstate.edu/sites/default/files/occrp/pdf/ccerr-findings-from-evaluations-of-the-implementation-of-multnomah-county-early-kindergarten-transition-program.pdf

Addressing the High Costs of Student Mobility,
http://hepg.org/hel-home/issues/29_2/helarticle/addressing-the-high-costs-of-student-mobility_563

Student Mobility: Helping Children Cope With a Moving Experience,
http://www.educationworld.com/a_curr/curr134.shtml#sthash.LEJRg2Vy.dpuf

Students on the Move: Reaching and Teaching Highly Mobile Children and Youth,
http://center.serve.org/nche/downloads/highly_mobile.pdf

A Revolving Door: Challenges and Solutions to Educating Mobile Students,
https://www.onefamilyinc.org/Blog/2011/09/26/a-revolving-door-challenges-and-solutions-to-educating-mobile-students/

Addressing School Adjustment Problems,
http://smhp.psych.ucla.edu/pdfdocs/adjustmentproblems.pdf

Schools Offering Service with a Smile,
http://www.educationworld.com/a_admin/admin/admin430.shtml

Making New Students Feel Welcome in Your Classroom,
http://www.scholastic.com/teachers/top-teaching/2015/01/making-new-students-feel-welcome-your-classroom

Does Your School's Atmosphere Shout "Welcome?",
http://www.educationworld.com/a_admin/admin/admin424.shtml

Moving Targets,
http://www.edweek.org/ew/articles/2001/04/04/29mobility.h20.html

Learning Together Case Studies,
http://www.learningtogether.com/sites/learningtogether.com/files/pdf/L2_CASE%20STUDIES%20%281%29.pdf

Make New Families Feel Welcome,
http://www.ptotoday.com/pto-today-articles/article/681-make-new-families-feel-welcome

Helping Newcomer Students Succeed in Secondary Schools and Beyond,
http://www.cal.org/resource-center/publications/helping-newcomer-students

Organizing a Successful Family Center in Your School,
http://fscp.dpi.wi.gov/sites/default/files/imce/fscp/pdf/fcsprntc.pdf

Serving Recent Immigrant Students Through School-Community Partnerships,
http://www.colorincolorado.org/article/serving-recent-immigrant-students-through-school-community-partnerships

Welcoming Immigrant Families and Students,
http://www.nea.org/assets/docs/hispanicfocus2011-2012.pdf

Ninth Grade Counts: Using Summer Bridge Programs to Strengthen the High School Transition,
https://www2.ed.gov/programs/slcp/ninthgradecounts/ninthgradecountssummer-bridgeguide.pdf

The Future of Children Journal Issue: Military Children and Families,
http://futureofchildren.org/publications/journals/article/index.xml?journalid=80&articleid=592&sectionid=4128&submit

Engaging Parents in Education: Lessons from Five Parental Information and Resource Centers,
http://www2.ed.gov/admins/comm/parents/parentinvolve/report_pg19.html

WelConnect App

As mentioned in Chapter 4, WelConnect is a mobile app designed to making the school transition process less stressful for families. It was created as part of the *Welcoming Practices* consortium at the University of Southern California (USC). *Welcoming Practices* collaborated with faculty and students in the USC Viterbi School of Engineering to develop and release the app.

WelConnect was made available to five military-connected school districts in San Diego and Riverside counties that experience high student mobility. The app, however, has wide potential to help any family that is relocating because of new jobs, immigration, financial hardship, or other reasons. Available on both Android and iOS devices, the app allows users to search for the local resources and programs they need near their local school, such as athletic programs, tutoring services, health care, or child care providers, and save them as favorites for easy reference. The resources are organized into four categories: district, school, community, and military.

Features

The app has four main tabs: featured resources, favorite resources, search resources and a profile (Figure Appx-B.1). The map component, which allows users to locate any program or resource, is part of the detailed resource information screen (Figure Appx-B.2). Contact information for any program or organization is also available.

A rating system is also integrated so users can provide feedback on community-based programs that might be helpful to other families (Figure Appx-B.3). Users can also flag whether a piece of information related to a resource is incorrect, such as a phone number or if the program no longer exists. This information is transmitted to

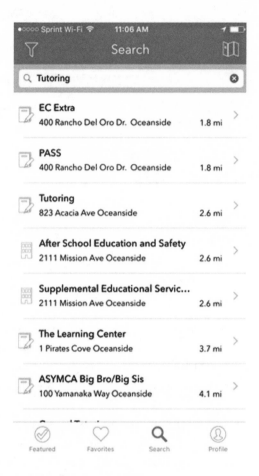

FIGURE APPX-B.1 This is how the resources appear on the app.

the tech team as well as to the school districts so they can fix the error and delete the flag. Finally, an administrative portal has been created and school district personnel were trained to update information related to programs within their district and schools.

Multiple Users

In addition to parents using the app to find resources or programs, teachers, school counselors, social workers, and other personnel can use the app to find district- or community-based programs that meet the needs of individual students.

"The WelConnect app has been a helpful resource for Fallbrook High School faculty and families," says Nicole Webb, who served as the school's parent center liaison.

FIGURE APPX-B.2 The map function helps users locate programs and services.

"I've used the app as a parent liaison to help students and their families, military and non-military, who are transitioning into Fallbrook High School. The app provides a one-stop location for an array of resources at your fingertips."

Local service providers that want to work in partnership with schools, such as after-school programs, tutoring centers, mental health organizations, youth sports, or arts programs, can also use the app to learn more about the schools and districts in their area. In communities near military bases, military school liaison officers can use the app to make sure children in military families are finding and receiving the services they need to be successful in school. "The WelConnect app is a valuable resource that helps give families immediate access to important school and community information," says Tina Archer, the military family advocate for the Chula Vista Elementary School District, one of the five districts to first use the app.

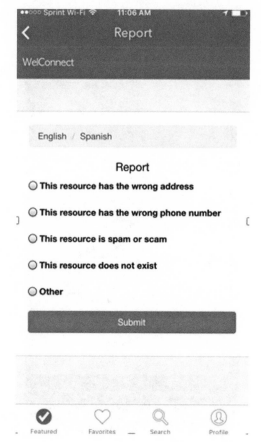

FIGURE APPX-B.3 This is the screen used to report a problem so administrators can correct the information.

Website

The app development team also created a WelConnect website (https://www.welconnect. org) that describes the features of the app and includes a Help Center where users can send messages that go directly to the app development team. The website provides tutorial videos on how to log in, search for resources, save them as favorites, find the location of a provider, and use the other features of the app. One video describes the app's benefits for community organizations, and the second video describes how the app can help parents and families.

Sample Surveys for Welcoming Newcomers

Here we provide examples of surveys that educators can use or adapt to learn about students' and parents' experiences in their new schools. These surveys were used in the *Welcoming Practices* consortium. Districts and schools can take some of the questions in this survey and come up with additional and different items that meet their needs.

Student Survey

(This survey was modified to leave out some of the information that only pertained to the *Welcoming Practices* consortium districts.)

Dear Student,
The aim of this survey is to learn from you, and understand how you felt as a new student in your school, and how you feel now.

The information you and other students provide will be used to inform district and school staff about how students feel and what they think about how districts and schools can improve the experiences of students in school, especially how they welcome new students. Of course, we never share any personal information, and all feedback that we provide does not reveal information on any individual students.

We invite you to participate in this 15-minute survey which will provide you with an opportunity to share your thoughts, feelings, and ideas with your school and district.

This survey is voluntary and anonymous. No identifying information will be asked or released. We thank you very much for taking the time to provide your feedback. What you have to say is very important!

In the following section, the school name is requested. (This is edited to be shorter and less technical).

1. What grade are you currently in?

2. What gender do you identify with?
    A. Male
    B. Female
    C. Decline to State

3. When did you enroll in your current school?
    A. This Year
    B. Last Year
    C. Two Years Ago
    D. Three or More Years Ago

4. Which of the following best describes your experience transitioning into your current school?
    A. I first enrolled in my current school at the beginning of a new school year.
    B. I first enrolled in my current school during the school year (not at the beginning of a new school year).

5. As far as you can remember, how many times have you changed schools due to a family move?

6. How active are you on the following social media networks (if at all)?

	Not At All	A Little (a Few Times a Month)	I Am Active (a Few Times a Week)	I Am Very Active (Daily)
Facebook	1	2	3	4
Twitter	1	2	3	4

7. Is anyone in your family currently serving in the military, and, if so, who (mark all that apply)?
    A. No one in my family is currently serving in the military.
    B. My father and/or stepfather is currently serving in the military.
    C. My mother and/or stepmother is currently serving in the military.
    D. My sibling and/or step-sibling is currently serving in the military.

8. Has anyone in your family previously served in the military, and, if so, who (mark all that apply)?

    A. No one in my family has previously served in the military.

    B. My father and/or stepfather previously served in the military (not currently serving).

    C. My mother and/or stepmother previously served in the military (not currently serving).

    D. My sibling and/or step-sibling previously served in the military (not currently serving).

9. Many students find moving to a new school and a new neighborhood a great opportunity to make new friends and have new experiences. Many others find the first few days and weeks in school quite challenging. We would like to ask you to share with us what happened to YOU, in your first days and weeks in this school.

    When I came to this school as a new student:

	Not at All	To Some Extent	To a Large Extent
The school helped me with my school work (when I needed help).	1	2	3
The school made it easy for me to transfer credits from my other schools.	1	2	3
I was assigned another student in school (a "buddy") to help me get to know the school.	1	2	3
I was given a tour of the school.	1	2	3
The school had a special reception for new students.	1	2	3
Students in this school greeted and welcomed me as a new student.	1	2	3
I was welcomed by a Student to Student (S2S), social club, or an ambassador program.	1	2	3
Many teachers knew my name right away.	1	2	3

10. When I came to this school as a new student, school staff provided me the information I needed on:

	Not at All	To Some Extent	To a Large Extent
Academic requirements	1	2	3
School rules and procedures	1	2	3
Opportunities for extracurricular activities	1	2	3
Opportunities to get involved in school social life and school events	1	2	3

11. Any other ways in which the school helped you when you entered this school?

12. What could the school have done more of to help you feel welcomed and part of the school?

13. How would you describe your first weeks and months as a new student in your current school?

	Strongly Disagree	Disagree	Neutral	Agree	Strongly Agree
I found new friends quickly.	1	2	3	4	5
I knew my way around the school within a few weeks.	1	2	3	4	5
I felt part of the school within a few weeks.	1	2	3	4	5
I was able to do well in my school work.	1	2	3	4	5
I felt quite lonely.	1	2	3	4	5

14. How do you feel as a student in your current school today?

	Strongly Disagree	Disagree	Neutral	Agree	Strongly Agree
I feel close to people at this school.	1	2	3	4	5
I am happy to be at this school.	1	2	3	4	5
I feel like I am part of this school.	1	2	3	4	5
I feel safe at this school.	1	2	3	4	5
Teachers at this school treat students fairly.	1	2	3	4	5

15. At my school, there is a teacher or some other adult who . . .

	Not at All True	A Little True	Pretty Much True	Very Much True
Really cares about me.	1	2	3	4
Tells me when I do a good job.	1	2	3	4
Notices me when I'm not there.	1	2	3	4
Wants me to do my best.	1	2	3	4
Listens to me when I have something to say.	1	2	3	4
Believes I will be a success.	1	2	3	4

16. I have at least one friend my own age . . .

	Not at All True	A Little True	Pretty Much True	Very Much True
Who really cares about me.	1	2	3	4
Who talks with me about my problems.	1	2	3	4
Who helps me when I'm having a hard time.	1	2	3	4
With whom I can have fun.	1	2	3	4

17. Please share with us any additional comments or ideas that you may have.

We Thank You Very Much for Your Participation!

Parent Survey

Dear Family,

As part of our efforts to listen to families and students, we are asking you to respond to this brief survey designed to learn about your experiences as new families to the school. Let us know both what you liked and what you think should be improved in how the school district and schools welcome new families and students. This information will be used anonymously to help change district and school policies so that each family feels welcomed when they come to the school. Please note that our independent team keeps your identity and responses confidential and will not share individual comments or reactions with the district and school or any personal information that you provide. However, any ideas you have will be shared anonymously to improve policy and practices.

I. Background Information

1. How many of your children attend school in THIS district?
    A. One
    B. Two
    C. Three
    D. Four children or more

2. Please indicate the gender, age, grade level, and school of your children (up to five children)

	Gender	Age	Grade Level	School
First (oldest) child				
Second				
Third				
Fourth				
Fifth				

3. How many different schools do your children attend?
    A. One school
    B. Two different schools
    C. Three different schools
    D. My children attend more than three different schools.

4. Which types of schools do your children attend? (you can mark more than one option)
   A. Pre-kindergarten
   B. Kindergarten
   C. Primary school
   D. Middle school
   E. High school

5. We will now ask you a couple of questions to help us improve the ways we communicate with your family in the future. Do you have Internet at home?
   A. Yes
   B. No

6. Do you own a smartphone?
   A. Yes
   B. No

7. If you own a smartphone, please indicate which type:
   A. iPhone
   B. Android (e.g., Samsung, LG)
   C. Windows
   D. Blackberry
   E. Other

8. In what language would you like to receive future information?
   A. English
   B. Spanish
   C. Other language

9. If other language, please tell us which language would you prefer.

10. When was the MOST RECENT time that you registered a child in this district?
    A. This year
    B. Last year
    C. Earlier

II. Registration

In this section, please refer to your most recent experience in registering a child to this district.

11. Where did you and your family relocate from?
    A. From outside the state of California
    B. From a different district in California
    C. From another school in this district
    D. This was the first school of our child.

12. Which of the following best describes your family (you may select more than one option)?
    A. Neither my spouse (or partner) nor I have served in the military.
    B. My spouse or partner and/or I are currently serving in the military.
    C. My spouse or partner and/or I are veterans.

13. Prior to registering your child/children, have you received information about the school or district?
    A. Yes
    B. No
    C. Don't know/don't remember

14. If yes, who provided this information (you may select more than on option)?
    A. School district
    B. School liaison officer
    C. Registrar
    D. Principal
    E. School or district secretary
    F. Families already in this school
    G. Other

15. How did you register your child/children (you may select more than one option)?
    A. Documents in the mail
    B. Online
    C. Electronic mail (email)
    D. In person
    E. Other

16. Please rate your level of agreement with the following statements related to the registration process:

	Strongly Disagree	Disagree	Neither Agree Nor Disagree	Agree	Strongly Agree	Not Applicable
The registration process was clearly explained to me.	1	2	3	4	5	6
Questions related to the registration process were answered in a timely manner.	1	2	3	4	5	6
The district/ school expressed an interest in understanding and meeting my family's needs throughout the registration process.	1	2	3	4	5	6
My interactions with the district/ school throughout the registration process were positive overall.	1	2	3	4	5	6
My child's school records and documents were received and processed in a timely manner.	1	2	3	4	5	6

17. Overall, how satisfied were you with the registration process?
   A. Very Dissatisfied
   B. Dissatisfied
   C. Neutral
   D. Satisfied
   E. Very Satisfied

III. Information on School and District Services and Resources

18. We would like to ask whether the district or school provided you with information on resources and services. We also ask you whether you are now interested in receiving information about these resources.

	District or school provided this information		I am interested in receiving this information	
	Yes	No	Yes	No
Academic requirements	1	2	1	2
Academic support programs (e.g., tutoring, mentoring, academic counseling, career planning)	1	2	1	2
Extracurricular activities/before- and after-school programs (e.g., child care, youth and recreation centers, athletic programs, social clubs)	1	2	1	2
Parent engagement opportunities (e.g., parent volunteer opportunities, PTA meetings, school events)	1	2	1	2
Community support programs in the local area (e.g., community resource centers, community service opportunities, local groups)	1	2	1	2

	District or school provided this information		I am interested in receiving this information	
	Yes	No	Yes	No
Health and wellness programs in the local area (e.g., fitness programs, nutrition workshops, community clinics)	1	2	1	2
Local mental health services (e.g., marriage and family counseling, hospital workshops, suicide prevention, PTSD support)	1	2	1	2
Legal services in the local area (e.g., legal counseling, immigration/visa counseling)	1	2	1	2
Financial services in the local area (e.g., financial literacy courses, employment services, housing services)	1	2	1	2
Programs and services for military-connected families (e.g., veteran support services, deployment services, resiliency programs, relocation assistance, support for homeless veterans, mental health services)	1	2	1	2
Local military installations (including child and family programs and the school liaison officer program)	1	2	1	2

IV. Welcoming Schools

19. Please rate your level of agreement with the following statements in regard to your child's school. Because you may have different experiences with different schools, we ask you to tell us about each of the schools that your children attend separately.

20. The name of the first school:

21. Describing the experiences with this school

	Strongly Disagree	Disagree	Neither Agree Nor Disagree	Agree	Strongly Agree
I felt welcomed by the school.	1	2	3	4	5
The school made us feel like we were part of the school community.	1	2	3	4	5
The school helped me connect to other families.	1	2	3	4	5
The school helped connect me to services and resources in the area.	1	2	3	4	5
My child felt welcomed by the school.	1	2	3	4	5
The school accommodated the needs of my child.	1	2	3	4	5
The school made my child feel like he/she was part of the school community.	1	2	3	4	5
The school helped my child connect with other students.	1	2	3	4	5
The school helped my child succeed in school.	1	2	3	4	5

22. Please share with us what the schools have done that made you feel welcome or unwelcome. If you have more than one child in different schools, please make suggestions for each school.

23. If you are a military family, did you feel welcome and respected in your child/children's school? Could you share your experiences?

24. Please share with us any questions, recommendations, and/or concerns in regard to how you registered and were welcomed by the school. If you have more than one child in different schools, please make suggestions for each school.

Research

Understanding what researchers have found about students transitioning between schools can better inform educators' efforts to support them and their families. This appendix provides examples of scientific, empirical studies that address issues of mobility and transition. These could serve as the beginning of thorough and updated reviews for students, scholars, professionals, and policymakers interested in this topic.

Alsem, M. W., Verhoef, M., Gorter, J. W., Langezaal, L. C. M, Visser-Meily, J. M., & Ketelaar, M. (2016). Parents' perceptions of the services provided to children with cerebral palsy in the transition from preschool rehabilitation to school-based services *Child: Care, Health and Development, 42*, 455–463.

This study focuses on the perceptions of 59 parents to children with cerebral palsy (CP) of the rehabilitative services their child received before and after the transition from preschool to school-based services. Parents' perceptions of preschool services were stable between the ages of 2.5 and 3.5 years, with a decline on several dimensions after transition. The authors conclude that the transition from preschool to school-based services for children with CP is associated with a decrease in parents' perception that families are at the center of the provision of rehabilitative services, independent of the type of school.

Carson, D., Esbensen, F., & Taylor, T. (2013). A longitudinal analysis of the relationship between school victimization and student mobility. *Youth Violence and Juvenile Justice, 11*, 275–295.

This study expands research on victimization at school by focusing on mobile youth. School mobility is of concern to both educators and practitioners and is associated with a number of harmful as well as beneficial outcomes (e.g., dropout and school failure, deviant behaviors, or increased test scores and grades). This research uses longitudinal data from a sample of approximately 2,000 youth to examine the effect of in-school victimization on school mobility and the consequences of school mobility on subsequent victimization. Findings from multilevel regression and change score analyses indicate that middle school youth who are victimized are more likely to change schools and experience less victimization at the new school.

Dauter, L., & Fuller, B. (2016). Student movement in social context: The influence of time, peers, and place. *American Educational Research Journal, 53,* 33–70. DOI: 10.3102/0002831215624981

Higher rates of school switching by students contribute to achievement disparities and are typically theorized as driven by attributes of individual pupils or families. In contrast, the neoclassical-economic account postulates that switching is necessary for competition among schools. The authors argue that both frames fail to capture social-referential and institutional comparisons that drive student mobility, hypothesizing that pupil mobility stems from the (a) student's time in school and grade; (b) student's race, class, and achievement relative to peers; (c) quality of schooling relative to nearby alternatives; and (d) proximity, abundance, and diversity of local school options. Propositions are tested with discrete-time hazard models using data from Los Angeles, including 6.5 million observations. They find the student's position relative to peers, relative school quality, and proximity to local alternatives contributes significantly to the likelihood of switching schools, beyond the effects of individual pupil or family attributes. Implications for understanding choice as a social-referential process within diverse organizational fields like urban education markets are discussed.

Evans, G., Yoo, M., & Sipple, J. (2010). The ecological context of student achievement: School building quality effects are exacerbated by high levels of student mobility. *Journal of Environmental Psychology, 30,* 239–244.

National reports, along with numerous statewide studies, indicate that the physical infrastructure of American schools is crumbling. At the same time, there is emerging evidence that school building quality matters for children's academic achievement. The authors integrate two separate literatures that have demonstrated that low school building quality as well as high rates of student mobility each contribute to reduced academic achievement by showing that these two variables statistically interact. Elementary school children in 511 New York City public schools have lower achievement scores if they attend schools of poor structural quality and with high rates of student mobility. The significant main and interactive effects of school building quality and student mobility on standardized test scores occur independently of socioeconomic and racial composition of the school.

Fiel, J., Haskins, A., & Turley, R. (2013). Reducing school mobility: A randomized trial of a relationship-building intervention. *American Educational Research Journal, 50,* 1188–1218.

Student turnover has many negative consequences for students and schools, and the high mobility rates of disadvantaged students may exacerbate inequality. Scholars have advised schools to reduce mobility by building and improving relationships with and among families, but such efforts are rarely tested rigorously. A cluster-randomized field experiment in 52 predominantly Hispanic elementary schools in San Antonio, Texas, and Phoenix, Arizona, tested whether student mobility in early elementary school was reduced through Families and Schools Together (FAST). FAST failed to reduce mobility overall but substantially reduced the mobility of black students, who were especially likely to change schools. Improved relationships among families help explain this finding.

Gasper, J., DeLuca, S., & Estacion, A. (2012). Switching schools: Revisiting the relationship between school mobility and high school dropout. *American Educational Research Journal, 49,* 487–519.

Youth who switch schools are more likely to demonstrate a wide array of negative behavioral and educational outcomes, including dropping out of high school. However, whether switching schools actually puts youth at risk for dropout is uncertain since youth who switch schools are similar to dropouts in their levels of prior school achievement and engagement, which suggests that switching schools may be part of the same long-term developmental process of disengagement that leads to dropping out. Using data from the National Longitudinal Survey of Youth 1997, this study uses propensity score matching to pair youth who switched high schools with similar youth who stayed in the same school. The authors find that although more than half the association between switching schools and dropping out is explained by observed characteristics *prior* to 9th grade, switching schools is still associated with dropping out.

Gillespie, B. (2013). Adolescent behavior and achievement, social capital, and the timing of geographic mobility. *Advances in Life Course Research, 18,* 223–233.

This paper examines the relationship between geographic mobility and adolescent academic achievement and behavior problems. Specifically, it addresses how the effects of moving differ by age and how social capital moderates the impact of moving on children (aged 6–15). Children's behavior problems and academic achievement test scores were compared across four survey waves of the National Longitudinal Survey of Youth (2000, 2002, 2004, and 2006) and matched to data from their mothers' reports from the National Longitudinal Survey of Youth 1979. The findings indicate that the negative behavioral effects of geographic mobility on adolescents are most pronounced for individuals relocating to a new city, county, or state as opposed to those moving locally (i.e., within the same city). Furthermore, as suggested by a life-course perspective, the negative effects of moving on behavior problems decrease as children get older. The results also show that several social capital factors moderate the effects of moving on behavior but not achievement.

Grigg, J. (2012). School enrollment changes and student achievement growth: A case study in educational disruption and continuity. *Sociology of Education, 85*, 388–404.

Student moves occur for many reasons, including both promotional transitions between educational levels and nonpromotional moves. Using panel data from students enrolled in grades 3 to 8 in the Metropolitan Nashville public schools during the implementation of a major change in school attendance policies, this article investigates the potential influence of four types of school changes, including promotional student mobility, on test score growth in reading and mathematics. All types of changes are associated with lower achievement growth during the year the enrollment change occurred, representing approximately 6% of expected annual growth, or 10 days of instruction. This incremental deficit is particularly concerning for disadvantaged students since they change schools more frequently. The results suggest that being new to a school does influence student achievement net of other factors; the results also imply that important social ties are ruptured when students change schools.

Hanushek, E. A., Kain, J. F., & Rivkin, S. G. (2004). Disruption versus Tiebout improvement: The costs and benefits of switching schools. *Journal of Public Economics, 88*, 1721–1746. DOI: 10.1016/S0047-2727(03)00063-X

Most students change schools at some point in their academic careers, but some change very frequently and some schools experience a great deal of turnover. Moves dictated by divorce, job loss, or similar events would be expected to disrupt academic progress, whereas "Tiebout" mobility—that is, a deliberate choice made by parents in order to achieve their goals, such as changing districts to pursue higher quality schools or better matches for their children—would generally be thought of as achievement-enhancing. The study is based on a database that tracks three cohorts of students in Texas. For each cohort, there are 200,000 students in more than 3,000 public schools. This paper disentangles the disruption effects of moves from changes in school quality. Importantly, it identifies the negative externality movers impose on other students. Student turnover is shown to entail a substantial cost for movers and non-movers alike. This cost appears to be larger for lower income and minority students who typically attend schools with much higher turnover.

Herbers, J., Reynolds, A., & Chen, C. (2013). Social mobility and developmental outcomes in young children. *Development and Psychopathology, 25*, 501–515.

School mobility has been shown to increase the risk of poor achievement, behavior problems, grade retention, and high school dropout. Using data over 25 years from the Chicago Longitudinal Study, the researchers investigated the unique risk of school moves on a variety of young adult outcomes including educational attainment, occupational prestige, depression symptoms, and criminal arrests. They also investigated how the timing of school mobility, whether earlier or later in the academic career, may differentially predict these outcomes over and above associated risks. Results indicate that students who experience more school changes between kindergarten and 12th grade are less likely to complete high school on time, complete fewer years of school, attain lower levels of occupational prestige, experience more symptoms of depression, and are more likely to be arrested as adults. Furthermore, the number of school moves predicted outcomes above and beyond associated risks such as residential mobility and family poverty. When timing of school mobility was examined, results indicated more negative outcomes associated with moves later, particularly between 4th and 8th grades.

Kim, H. K., & Leve, L. D. (2011). Substance use and delinquency among middle school girls in foster care: A three-year follow-up of a randomized controlled trial. *Journal of Consulting and Clinical Psychology, 79*, 740–750.

This study evaluated the efficacy of the Middle School Success (MSS) intervention for reducing substance use and delinquency among 100 girls in foster care during their transition to middle school in order to prevent delinquency, substance use, and related problems. This study is a follow-up to a previous study of these girls. The authors report that, 36 months after baseline, girls in the intervention showed significantly lower levels of substance use compared with girls in the control group. Further analyses indicated significant indirect effects of the intervention through increased prosocial behaviors that led to decreased internalizing and externalizing symptoms and then to lower levels of substance use. For delinquency, the intervention had positive effects mainly through increased prosocial skills. The authors conclude that the study highlights the importance of providing preventive intervention services during this period of transition to girls in foster care.

Lane, K. L. Oakes, W. P., Carter, E. E., & Messenger, M. (2015). Examining behavioral risk and academic performance for students transitioning from elementary to middle school. *Journal of Positive Behavior Interventions, 17*, 39–49.

This study investigated how behavioral risk, evident in the elementary years of 74 5th-grade students, impacts students. The authors followed these students in their transition from elementary to middle school. They examined how student risk status shifts as students transitioned from elementary to middle school and whether these shifts in risk were comparable with the shifts in risk occurring *within* the 5th-grade year. There was a positive relation between special education status and initial behavioral risk when compared with risk evident during 6th grade. Findings suggest a strong relation between grade point average and course failures with behavioral risk in 6th grade.

Raudenbush, S. W., Jean, M., & Art, E. (2011). Year-by-year and cumulative impacts of attending a high-mobility elementary school on children's mathematics achievement in Chicago, 1995 to 2005. In G. J. Duncan & R. J. Murnane (Eds.), *Whither opportunity? Rising inequality, schools, and children's life chances* (pp. 359–375). New York: Russell Sage Foundation.

Urban families living in poverty frequently move, usually over short distances. Moves often trigger school changes. This contributed chapter asks whether attending a school characterized by high levels of student mobility depresses learning. In particular, the chapter asks to what extent influxes of new students during the school year reduces students' mathematics achievement during the elementary school years, whether they accumulate over time, and whether they vary as a function of student background.

The study is based on secondary analysis of large datasets of students in Chicago. The findings indicate that African-American students and students in high-poverty schools are at the greatest risk of attending schools with high within-year in-migration. There are negative effects of within-year in-migrations, and they are relevant for both mobile and "stable" students. The authors conclude that high student mobility exacts a small but real cost on the general student population and contributes modestly to racial inequality in mathematics achievement.

Schmitt, S. A., Finders, J. K., & McClelland, M. M. (2015). Residential mobility, inhibitory control, and academic achievement in preschool. *Early Education and Development, 26*, 189–208. DOI: 10.1080/10409289.2015.975033

This study investigated the direct effects of residential mobility on children's inhibitory control and academic achievement during the preschool year. It also explored fall inhibitory control and academic skills as mediators linking residential mobility and spring achievement. Participants included 359 preschool children (49% female) studied in the fall and spring of the preschool year (73% were enrolled in Head Start). Residential mobility was significantly and negatively associated with fall inhibitory control and fall math skills and literacy. Significant indirect effects of mobility were found for spring math skills and literacy through inhibitory control and fall achievement. Specifically, the negative relation between mobility and spring math skills and literacy was partially explained by lower scores on fall inhibitory control and academic skills.

Schwartz, A. E., Stiefel, L., & Chalico, L. (2007). *The multiple dimensions of student mobility and implications for academic performance: Evidence from New York City elementary and middle school students.* A report for the New York Educational Finance Research Consortium.

The purpose of this study is threefold: to develop measures of alternative types of student mobility; to document the magnitudes of each type of mobility in aggregate and by student income, race/ethnicity, and immigrant status; and to analyze how mobility of different types affects student academic performance. The main findings of this study are that there is considerable mobility into New York City primary schools, considerable inter-year mobility for students staying in the district, and some intra-year mobility. Furthermore, the authors found that, over time, between 6% and 7% enter into each grade of a cohort, and students move several times over their schooling history.

Selya A. S., Engel-Rebitzer, E., Dierker, L., Stephen, E., Rose, J., Coffman, D. L., & Otis, M. (2016). The causal effect of student mobility on standardized test performance: A case study with possible implications for accountability mandates within the Elementary and Secondary Education Act. *Frontiers of Psychology, 7,* 1–10.

There is strong evidence to suggest that mobile students experience significant problems in multiple areas. But because mobile students tend to have characteristics that are very different from those of students who change schools less often, it remains unclear whether mobility has an effect on student performance above and beyond these pre-existing differences. The authors used a statistical technique, Propensity Score Matching, that aims to control background variables that may influence the outcomes of mobility, thus getting closer to understanding the causal effects of mobility. The study is based on 319 students in one suburban school in Connecticut. Analyses showed that mobility was associated with lower performance in writing. This trend was only significant among those who were ineligible for free/reduced lunches, but not among eligible students. The authors discuss the findings in light of the limited sample and their relevance to the Every Student Succeeds Act.

Theriot, M., & Dupper, D. (2010). Student discipline problems and the transition from elementary to middle school. *Education and Urban Society, 42,* 205–222.

The transition from elementary to middle school is difficult for many students. However, the association between such transitions and changes in the types and frequencies of student discipline problems has not been adequately investigated. Using data from two school years, infractions and dispositions for all 5th-grade students ($N = 4,196$) from one school district are followed from the final year of elementary school through the first year of middle school. Results show a substantial increase in reported student discipline problems and the use of in-school suspension in middle school. This increase is most dramatic for subjectively defined infractions like "class disturbance" and "failure to follow rules" compared to more concrete, objective infractions.

U.S. Government Accountability Office. (2010). *K-12 Education: Many challenges arise in educating students who change schools frequently.* Washington, DC: US Government Accountability Office. http://www.gao.gov/products/GAO-11-40

Economic downturn, with foreclosures and homelessness, may be increasing student mobility. The US Government Accountability Office (GAO) was asked: What are the numbers and characteristics of students who change schools, and what are the reasons students change schools? What is known about the effects of mobility on student outcomes, including academic achievement, behavior, and other outcomes? What challenges do student mobility present for schools in meeting the educational needs of students who change schools? What key federal programs are schools using to address the needs of mobile students? The GAO analyzed federal survey data, interviewed US Department of Education officials, conducted site visits at eight schools in six school districts, and reviewed federal laws and existing research.

According to national survey data, students who change schools most frequently (four or more times) represented about 13% of all kindergarten through 8th-grade students, and they were disproportionately poor, African-American, and from families that did not own their home. About 11.5% of schools also had high rates of mobility—more than 10% of K-8 students left by the end of the school year. These schools, in addition to serving a mobile population, had larger percentages of students who were low-income, received special education, and had limited English proficiency. With respect to academic achievement, students who change schools more frequently tend to have lower scores on standardized reading and math tests and drop out of school at higher rates than their less mobile peers.

Voight, A., Shinn, M., & Nation, M. (2012). The longitudinal effects of residential mobility on the academic achievement of urban elementary and middle school students. *Educational Researcher, 41,* 385–392. DOI: 10.3102/0013189X12442239

Residential stability matters to a young person's educational development, and the present housing crisis has disrupted the residential stability of many families. This study uses latent growth-curve modeling to examine how changing residences affects math and reading achievement from 3rd through 8th grade among a sample of urban elementary and middle school students. Results show that residential moves in the early elementary years have a negative effect on math and reading achievement in 3rd grade and a negative effect on the trajectory of reading scores thereafter. Furthermore, there is a negative contemporaneous effect of mobility on math scores in 3rd through 8th grade but no such contemporaneous effect on reading scores.

Waters, S., Lester, L., & Cross, D. (2014). How does support from peers compare with support from adults as students transition to secondary school? *Journal of Adolescent Health, 54,* 543–549.

This study sought to determine from whom young people receive support before the transition period. Data were collected from 1,974 primary school students prior to the transition and again in Term 1 of the first year of secondary school. Students were asked about their expectation of the transition as well as their support from peers, family, and the school. Peer, school, and family supports all predicted positive student transition experiences. When in 7th grade and considering all predictors together, a high level of perceived peer support was the most significant predictor of an expectation of an easy or somewhat easy transition. In 8th grade, again after considering all sources of support, parental presence was the most significant protective predictor of an easy or somewhat easy transition experience. Students who expect and experience a positive transition to secondary school are generally well-supported by their peers, school, and family. The most stable influence for young people over the transition period is the presence of families before and after school, and future intervention efforts to support young people during transition need to build support from families.

Welsh, R., Duque, M., & McEachin, A. (2016). School choice, student mobility, and school quality: Evidence from post-Katrina New Orleans. *Education Finance and Policy, 11,* 150–176.

This paper analyzes student mobility between and within the various sectors and school types using a multinomial framework in post-Hurricane Katrina New Orleans. The authors find rates of student mobility in post-Katrina New Orleans to be similar to other traditional urban school districts. Results indicate that high-achieving students switch to high-quality schools whereas low-achieving students transfer to low-quality schools. It is clear that some students are taking advantage of the ability to choose a high-quality educational option, although many students are still not doing so.

Whipple, S., Evans, G., & Barry, R. (2010). An ecological perspective on cumulative school and neighborhood risk factors related to achievement. *Journal of Applied Developmental Psychology, 31,* 422–427.

Most educational reform programs, including No Child Left Behind, operate from the perspective that gaps in academic achievement can be reduced by improvements in the educational process directed by school administrators and teachers. This perspective ignores the ecological context in which underachieving schools are typically embedded. Using a developmental approach, the study shows that school-wide achievement of elementary school children in New York City is better characterized by the accumulation of multiple risk factors within schools and within the neighborhoods where they are situated. School risk factors include teacher experience, teacher and student mobility, teacher absences, and school building quality. Neighborhood risk factors include proportion in poverty, parental educational attainment, proportion of single parents, housing quality, residential crowding, and neighborhood deterioration. Cumulative risk within each of these ecological domains, as well as their interaction, is significantly associated with school-wide achievement.

Xu, Z., Hannaway, J., & D'Souza, S. (2009). Student transience in North Carolina: The effect of school mobility on student outcomes using longitudinal data. *National Center for Analysis of Longitudinal Data in Education Research (CALDER), Working Paper No. 82.* http://www.caldercenter.org/publications/student-transience-north-carolinathe-effect-school-mobility-student-outcomes-using

This paper describes the school mobility rates for elementary and middle school students in North Carolina and attempts to estimate the effect of school mobility on the performance of different groups of students. School mobility is defined as changing schools at times that are non-promotional (e.g., moving from middle to high school). The study uses detailed administrative data on North Carolina students and schools from 1996 to 2005 and follows four cohorts of 3rd-graders for six years each. School mobility rates were highest for minority and disadvantaged students. School mobility rates for Hispanic students declined across successive cohorts but increased for black students. Findings on effects were most pronounced in math. School mobility hurt the math performance of black and Hispanic students but not the math performance of white students. School mobility improved the reading performance of white and more advantaged students but had no effect on the reading performance of minority students. "Strategic" school moves (cross-district) benefitted or had no effect on student performance, but "reactive" moves (within district) hurt all groups of students. White and Hispanic students were more likely to move to a higher quality school whereas black students were more likely to move to a lower quality school. The negative effects of school mobility increased with the number of school moves.

Notes

INTRODUCTION

1. www.hfrp.org
2. http://www.schoolclimate.org
3. http://www.casel.org
4. https://www.aspeninstitute.org/programs/national-commission-on-social-emotional-and-academic-development/
5. https://people.clas.ufl.edu/espelage/
6. http://www.cehd.umn.edu/icd/people/faculty/Masten.html
7. http://studentmobility.net
8. http://www2.ed.gov/policy/elsec/leg/esea02/pg116.html
9. Interview.
10. http://www.ccsso.org/News_and_Events/Press_Releases/Texas_Teacher_Named_2015_National_Teacher_of_the_Year.html
11. http://www.sjhumanitas.org
12. Interview.

CHAPTER 1

1. Rumberger, R. W., Larson, K. A., Ream, R. K., & Palardy, G. J. (1999). The educational consequences of mobility for California students and schools. Berkeley, CA: Policy Analysis for California Education (PACE).
2. Engec, 2006; Rumberger, 2003.
3. Engec, N. (2006). Relationship between mobility and student performance and behavior. *Journal of Educational Research*, 99(3), 167-178; Rumberger, R. W. (2003). Causes and consequences of student mobility. *Journal of Negro Education*, 72(1), 6–21.
4. Bradshaw, Sudhinaraset, Mmari, & Blum, 2010; Branz-Spall, Rosenthal, & Wright, 2003; Cutuli et al., 2013; Fantuzzo, LeBeouf, Chen, Rouse, & Culhane, 2012; Hagan, Macmillan, & Wheaton, 1996; US Government Accountability Office, 2001.
5. Conger, D., & Reback, A. (2001). *How children's foster care experiences affect their education*. New York: Vera Institute of Justice.
6. Xu, Z., Hannaway, J., & D'Souza, S. (2009). *Student transience in North Carolina: The effect of school mobility on student outcomes using longitudinal data*. National Center for Analysis of Longitudinal Data in Education Research (CALDER), Working Paper no. 82. CALDER American Institutes for Research. Washington, DC.

7. Rennie Center for Education Research & Policy. (2011). *A revolving door: Challenges and solutions to educating mobile students.* Cambridge, MA: Rennie Center for Education Research & Policy.

8. Eadie, S., Eisner, R., Miller, B., & Wolf, L. (2013). Student mobility patterns and achievement in Wisconsin: Report prepared for the Wisconsin Department of Public Instruction. Madison, WI: University of Wisconsin-Madison Robert M. La Follette School of Public Affairs; Hanushek, E. A., Kain, J. F., & Rivkin, S. G. (2004). Disruption versus tiebout improvement: The costs and benefits of switching schools. *Journal of Public Economics*, 88(1721–1746); Offenberg, R. (2004). Inferring Adequate Yearly Progress of Schools from student achievement in highly mobile communities. *Journal of Education for Students Placed at Risk*, 9(4), 337–355.

9. Alexander, K. L., Entwisle, D. R., & Dauber, S. L. (1996). Children in motion: School transfers and elementary school performance. *Journal of Educational Research*, 90(1), 3–12.

10. Hanushek et al., 2004.

11. https://nces.ed.gov/programs/coe/pdf/coe_cfa.pdf

12. Burkam, D. T., Lee, V. E., & Dwyer, J. (2009). *School mobility in the early elementary grades: Frequency and impact from nationally-representative data.* Paper presented at the Workshop on the Impact of Mobility and Change on the Lives of Young Children, Schools, and Neighborhoods, Washington, DC.; Gruman, D. H., Harachi, T. W., Abbott, R. D., Catalano, R. F., & Fleming, C. B. (2008). Longitudinal effects of student mobility on three dimensions of elementary school engagement. *Child Development*, 79(6), 1833–1852; Mehana, M., & Reynolds, A. J. (2004). School mobility and achievement: A meta-analysis. *Children and Youth Services Review*, 26, 93-119; US Government Accountability Office. (2010). K-12 Education: Many challenges arise in educating students who change schools frequently. Washington, DC: US Government Accountability Office.

13. Grigg, J. (2012). School enrollment changes and student achievement growth: A case study in educational disruption and continuity. *Sociology of Education, 85*(4), 388-404.

14. Hanushek et al., 2004.

15. Mehana & Reynolds, 2004.

16. Raudenbush, S. W., Jean, M., & Art, E. (2011). Year-by-year and cumulative impacts of attending a high-mobility elementary schoolon children's mathematics achievement in Chicago, 1995 to 2005. In G. J. Duncan & R. J. Murnane (Eds.), *Whither opportunity? Rising inequality, schools, and children's life chances* (pp. 359–375). New York, NY: Russell Sage Foundation.

17. http://studentmobility.net

18. Simpson, G. A., & Fowler, M. G. (1994). Geographic mobility and children's emotional/behavioral adjustment and school functioning. *Pediatrics*, 93(2), 303–309.

19. Gruman, et al., 2008.

20. Gottfried, M. A. (2011). Absent peers in elementary years: The negative classroom effects of unexcused absences on standardized testing outcomes. *Teachers College Record*, 113(8), 1597–1632.

21. Minneapolis Public Schools. (1998). A report from the Kids Mobility Project. Minneapolis, MN: Minneapolis Public Schools, Hennepin County, University of Minnesorta CURA and CAREI, The Family Housing Fund; Parke, C. S., & Kanyongo, G. Y. (2012). Student attendance, mobility, and mathematics achievement. *Journal of Educational Research*, 105(3), 161–175.

22. Lee, V. E., & Burkam, D. T. (2003). Dropping out of high school: The role of school organization and structure. *American Educational Research Journal, 40*(2), 353–393; Rumberger, R. W., & Larson, K. A. (1998). Student mobility and the increased risk of high school dropout. *American Journal of Education, 107*(1), 1–35.

23. Bradshaw, C. P., Sudhinaraset, M., Mmari, K., & Blum, R. W. (2010). School transitions among military adolescents: A qualitative study of stress and coping. *School Psychology Review, 39*(1), 84–105.

24. Vernberg, E. (1990). Experience with peers following relocation during early adolescence. *American Journal of Orthopsychiatry, 60*(3), 466–472.

25. Haynie, D. L., & South, S. J. (2005). Residential mobility and adolescent violence. *Social Forces*, 84(1), 361–374.

26. Engec, N. (2006). Relationship between mobility and student performance and behavior. *Journal of Educational Research, 99*(3), 167–178; Simpson, G. A., & Fowler, M. G. (1994). Geographic mobility and children's emotional/behavioral adjustment and school functioning. *Pediatrics, 93*(2), 303–309.

27. Simpson & Fowler, 1994.
28. Grigg, 2012.
29. Kim, H. K., & Leve, L. D. (2011). Substance use and delinquency among middle school girls in foster care: A three year follow-up of a randomized controlled trial. *Journal of Consulting Clinical Psychology, 79*(6), 740–750.
30. Alspaugh, J. W. (1998). Achievement loss associated with the transition to middle school and high school. *Journal of Educational Research, 92*(1), 20–25.
31. Rockoff, J., & Lockwood, J. R. (2010). Stuck in the middle: Impacts of grade configuration in public schools. *Journal of Public Economics, 94*(11–12), 1051–1061.

CHAPTER 2
1. Interview.
2. http://www.communityresearchpartners.org/portfolios/ohio-student-mobility-research/
3. http://www.renniecenter.org/research/RevolvingDoor_MobileStudents.pdf
4. https://news.vanderbilt.edu/2015/03/04/mobility-in-tn-achievement-school-district-focus-of-new-study/
5. https://www2.ed.gov/about/inits/ed/implementation-support-unit/tech-assist/state-rules-for-linking-student-and-teacher.pdf
6. Interview
7. http://www.farmworkerfamily.org/50mile-regulation/

CHAPTER 3
1. http://www.hanoverresearch.com/2013/09/13/k-12-leadership-digest-september-2013-newsletter/
2. https://buildingcapacity.usc.edu/files/2015/04/Welcoming-Practices-Technical-Report-2015-2016.pdf
3. Interview.
4. Interview.
5. Interview.
6. http://developingchild.harvard.edu/science/key-concepts/resilience/
7. O'Brien, A. M. (2007). The effect of mobility on the academic achievement of military dependent children and their civilian peers. Peabody College for Teachers of Vanderbilt University (87 pages). AAT 3263831.

CHAPTER 4
1. Interview.
2. https://www.schoolwebmasters.com
3. https://www.welconnect.org
4. https://www.youtube.com/channel/UCINZVSLLXKRlSN_lnyHvI8Q
5. http://opelikaschools.org or http://www.opelikaschools.org/apps/video/watch.jsp?v=10020253
6. http://www.newtrier.k12.il.us/Audiences/New_Students/Ask_Transition_Coordinator/
7. Interview.
8. Dixon, B. (2012). *Social media for school leaders: A comprehensive guide to getting the most out of Facebook, Twitter, and other essential web tools.* San Francisco: Jossey-Bass.
9. Interview.
10. Interview.
11. http://news.stanford.edu/news/2014/november/texting-literacy-tips-111714.html
12. http://www.edpartnerships.org/sites/default/files/events/2015/02/NCCEP-Capacity-Building%20Txt%20for%20Success%20WV.pdf
13. Interview.

CHAPTER 5
1. https://www.hartfordschools.org/the-welcome-center/
2. Interview.
3. http://archive.constantcontact.com/fs155/1109130245016/archive/1118710891781.html

4. http://www.r2lp.org/r2lp-and-providence-schools-announce-3-million-grant-to-strengthen-family-engagement/

5. Interview.

6. Interview.

7. Interview.

8. Interview.

9. Interview.

10. Interview.

11. http://www.militarychild.org/parents-and-students/programs/student-2-student

12. Interview.

13. http://www.tolerance.org/supplement/newcomers-club

14. http://archive.constantcontact.com/fs022/1109130245016/archive/1109271259353.html

15. Interview.

16. http://www.educationworld.com/a_admin/admin/admin424.shtml

17. http://www.cms.k12.nc.us/parents/ParentUniv/Pages/default.aspx

18. Interview.

19. http://www.goodtherapy.org/blog/middle-school-intervention-girls-0807122

20. Wilkins, J., & Bost, L. W. (2016). Dropout prevention in middle and high schools from research to practice. *Intervention in School and Clinic, 51*(5), 267–275.

CHAPTER 6

1. https://www.naesp.org

2. http://www.cayl.org

3. https://www.wkkf.org/what-we-do/overview

4. http://www.readyfreddy.org/for-schools-and-communities/materials/

5. http://www.hfrp.org/family-involvement/publications-resources/a-new-approach-to-transitions-welcoming-families-and-their-ideas-into-kindergarten-classrooms

6. http://www.pthvp.org

7. Interview

8. http://www.hfrp.org/family-involvement/publications-resources/kindergarten-home-visit-project

9. http://health.oregonstate.edu/sites/default/files/occrp/pdf/ccerr-findings-from-evaluations-of-the-implementation-of-multnomah-county-early-kindergarten-transition-program.pdf

10. https://www.scholastic.com/teachers/blog-posts/brian-smith/successful-staggered-start-days-kindergarten/

11. http://www.pacer.org/parent/php/php-c160.pdf

CHAPTER 7

1. http://www.search-institute.org/content/40-developmental-assets-adolescents-ages-12-18

2. Interview.

3. https://www.amle.org/BrowsebyTopic/WhatsNew/WNDet/TabId/270/ArtMID/888/ArticleID/279/Culture-of-Connectedness-through-Advisory.aspx

4. http://oregongearup.org/resources/toolkits

5. http://www.boomerangproject.com

6. Interview.

CHAPTER 8

1. https://www.stephencovey.com

2. Interview.

3. http://www.catapultlearning.com/be-our-guest-re-imagining-parents-as-disney-would/

4. http://www.disabilityscoop.com/2013/09/03/schools-obligated-ieps/18630/

CHAPTER 9

1. http://www.treehouseforkids.org
2. http://www.ncpublicschools.org/docs/curriculum/home/transitions.pdf
3. Interview.
4. Interview.
5. http://palprogram.ucsd.edu
6. http://aacfoundation.com
7. https://www.irco.org

CHAPTER 10

1. http://www.attendanceworks.org/wordpress/wp-content/uploads/2014/09/Absenses-Add-Up_September-3rd-2014.pdf
2. http://www.attendanceworks.org/wordpress/wp-content/uploads/2014/08/Positive-Priority-Outreach-Toolkit_081914.pdf
3. http://www.learnlead.org/perfectly-punctual-campaign/
4. http://dc.cod.edu/cgi/viewcontent.cgi?article=1370&context=essai
5. http://www.usc.edu/vh/buildingcapacityarchive/Preventive%20Medicine%20Article%20bullying%20weapons-main.pdf
6. http://checkandconnect.umn.edu/implementation/options_funding.html
7. Interview.
8. http://www.rwjf.org/en/library/articles-and-news/2012/04/can-a-game-of-tag-help-combat-bullying.html
9. http://www.playworks.org
10. http://www.peacefulplaygrounds.com
11. Interview.
12. http://www.learningtogether.com/sites/learningtogether.com/files/pdf/L2_CASE%20STUDIES%20%281%29.pdf

CHAPTER 11

1. http://www.militarychild.org/public/upload/images/MCEC_Quick_Checklist_for_School_Moves.pdf
2. https://www.military.com/spouse/military-education/military-children-education/an-exit-interview-helps-kids-pcs.html
3. http://www.teachingsuccess.co.nz/help-students-transition/

Index

Page numbers followed by *b, f,* or *t* indicate boxes, figures, or tables, respectively.